BREAKING NEW GROUND ON THE GLOBAL STAGE:
MEMOIRS OF KUWAIT'S FIRST WOMAN AMBASSADOR

Breaking New Ground on the Global Stage

*Memoirs of Kuwait's
First Woman Ambassador*

BY NABEELA AL MULLA

MODERN MEMOIRS, INC.
Amherst, Massachusetts

The thoughts, reflections, and opinions expressed in this book are those of the author, based upon her personal recollections and research. The author takes full and sole responsibility for all of the contents, including text and images, and regrets any aspect of the content that might be construed as injurious to a party mentioned, implied, or referred to.

All photos are from the author's personal collection, except where indicated. Every effort has been made to secure permissions to reprint others' proprietary content, and any necessary corrections will be made in future reprints of this book should the author be alerted to inadvertent errors or omissions.

A scan of the author's article, "The Humanitarian Crisis in Syria: How It All Started," first published in *New Europe*, February 2013, is reprinted here as her own copyrighted material. All other reprinted letters and documents are public records or are the property of the author.

Cover design by Nicole Miller
ISBN: 979-8-9891183-7-3 softcover edition
To contact the author: Nabeela.Book@gmail.com

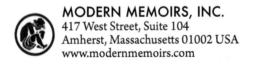

MODERN MEMOIRS, INC.
417 West Street, Suite 104
Amherst, Massachusetts 01002 USA
www.modernmemoirs.com

To Mother

Badriya Khaled Al-Ghuneim, circa 1934

CONTENTS

GLOSSARY OF ACRONYMS

USED IN THIS BOOK

ACRS   Arms Control and Regional Security

ANC   African National Congress

AUB   American University of Beirut

BOG   Board of Governors of the IAEA

CEDAW   Convention on the Elimination of All Forms of Discrimination Against Women

DARP   Delegation for Relations with the Arab Peninsula

DPRK   Democratic People's Republic of Korea (North Korea)

E3   France, Germany, United Kingdom

EU3+3 China, France, Germany, Russia, United Kingdom, United States. (Also known as P5+1)

EU   European Union

FBIS   Foreign Broadcast Information Service

GCC   Gulf Cooperation Council

IAEA   International Atomic Energy Agency

ICI   Istanbul Cooperation Initiative

IPU   Inter-Parliamentary Union

KFAED   Kuwait Fund for Arab Economic Development

KISR   Kuwait Institute for Scientific Research

MESA   Middle East and South Asia

NAC   North Atlantic Council

NATO   North Atlantic Treaty Organization

NPT   Non-Proliferation Treaty

NTI   Nuclear Threat Initiative

OAU   Organization of African Unity

OCHA   Office for the Coordination of Humanitarian Affairs at the United Nations

OIC   Organization of Islamic Cooperation

OPEC   Organization of the Petroleum Exporting Countries

P5+1   UNSC Permanent Members plus Germany. (Also known as EU3+3)

PLO   Palestine Liberation Organization

R2P   Responsibility to Protect, a component of the UN's Agenda for Peace

SADC   South African Development Community

TBTO   Test Ban Treaty Organization

UNAMI   United Nations Assistance Mission for Iraq

UNEP   United Nations Environment Programme

UNFICYP   United Nations Peacekeeping Force in Cyprus

UNIFIL   United Nations Interim Force in Lebanon

UNIIMOG   United Nations Iran-Iraq Military Observer Group

UNIKOM   United Nations Iraq-Kuwait Observation Mission

UNITAF Unified Task Force

UNMOVIC   United Nations Monitoring and Verification Commission

WHO   World Health Organization

In the 1960s, the State of Kuwait's early days were marked by jubilation and apprehension in equal measure. Kuwait achieved independence on 19 June 1961 under the reign of Sheikh Abdullah Al-Salim Al-Sabah. While concern arose due to Iraqi threats, a sense of urgency for viable government and public institutions to replace historic reliance on British administration also pervaded the country. Immediate needs included the establishment of a functioning Foreign Affairs office, if only to elicit recognition of the fledgling Gulf nation and seek membership in the United Nations.

The Secretary of Government, my late brother Bader Al Mulla, was delegated the responsibilities of signing letters seeking recognition and asking the Security Council to discuss ominous threats by Iraq. Bader was pulled out of his undergraduate studies in the United Kingdom in 1955 to follow in the footsteps of our father, Abdullah Al Mulla, and grandfather Saleh Al Mulla, who had successively served as Secretary of Government to the Amirs of Kuwait since 1906, starting with Sheikh Mubarak Al-Sabah.

Kuwait's new government initially faced a serious shortfall of foreign-affairs expertise and manpower. Given the close-knit relationships within Kuwaiti society, it drew upon prominent personalities to serve as ambassadors and officials in the Foreign Ministry. My maternal uncle Khalifa Khaled Al-Ghuneim was selected by Sheikh Abdullah Al-Salim Al-Sabah to be his first envoy to the United Kingdom.

Meanwhile, in October 1961 the Secretary of Government merged with the new Department of Foreign Affairs, with Sheikh Sabah Al-Salim Al-Sabah at the helm. In January 1962, Sheikh Sabah Al-Salim Al-Sabah was then named the first Minister of Foreign Affairs of the State of Kuwait. He served in that capacity until February 1963 and was succeeded by Sheikh Sabah Al-Ahmad Al-Sabah, who held that position for forty years until 2003, making him the second longest serving Foreign Minister.

During the course of my own decades-long diplomatic career, I have been fortunate to work for long periods under the guidance of Sheikh Sabah Al-Ahmad Al-Sabah, as well as that of Sheikh Salim Sabah Al-Salim Al-Sabah, and their successors Sheikh Dr. Mohammed Sabah Al-Salim Al-Sabah and Sheikh Sabah Al-Khaled Al-Sabah.

Some years ago, I toyed with the idea of writing the history of my family, but this was a feat accomplished by my diligent niece Shaimaa, who in 2023 published a well-documented book entitled *Al-Mulla: In the Realm of History and Politics,* concerning three Al Mulla Secretaries of Government—my grandfather, father, and brother. I decided to take a different angle with this memoir. Here, I aim to register my own narrative and experiences. I obtained from the UN archives some letters signed by my brother on behalf of Sheikh Abdullah Al-Salim Al-Sabah that were previously seized during Iraq's 1990 invasion. Those letters are included in the annex of this book, as few people are aware of the nascent history of the Kuwait Foreign Ministry. It is astounding to think how far it has come.

It has now been over six decades since independence and the Foreign Ministry's tumultuous beginning. Kuwait is blessed with a professional team of men and women educated and trained in the art and conduct of foreign policy. I owe it to this institution that I have served for over three decades and to the younger generation to shed some light on my own experience.

Ambassador Nabeela Al Mulla
Kuwait, 2024

Formative Years

> *It is not possible for me to make a better gift than to offer the opportunity of understanding in the shortest time all that I have learnt in so many years.*
>
> —Machiavelli, *The Prince*

"Presumptuous." This was the word the American professor scribbled on my thesis proposal to study nuclear non-proliferation at the American University of Beirut (AUB) in late 1969. A word that had never crossed my mind and certainly did not define me when I first joined AUB.

The university itself was an academic institution of great standing, and Beirut, the home to many leaders in the Arab world at that time. AUB was the alma mater of the first Kuwaiti graduate, my uncle, Khalifa Khaled Al-Ghuneim, class of 1944. Truth be told, however, despite its reputation and allure, AUB was not my first choice. When my application to my top pick, Oxford University, was not considered due to my being only sixteen years old at the time, the iconic British historian Elizabeth Monroe advised me to do an A-level, and my brother Anwar even encouraged me to join him in the United States. I settled on Plan B and the relative comfort of staying closer to home that attending AUB would grant me. I enrolled at AUB in 1964, ready to start the next chapter of my life in the beautiful political melting pot of Beirut, and completely unaware of the path on which I was about to embark.

I had options not normally afforded to others with a similar upbringing, due to my family's keen interest in my education and the exposure to life that they afforded me. I initially registered as a science student, planning to continue in a field I had thoroughly enjoyed in high school and toying with the idea of studying medicine, to follow in the footsteps of my accomplished sisters. One, Najeeba, was the first female doctor in Kuwait, and the other, Lateefa, the first female Kuwaiti radiographer. I even considered petroleum engineering but was dismayed to learn that women were not admitted to the AUB School of Engineering, something that would not change until 1967. Ultimately, however, I found the science classes intellectually unstimulating, and they quickly became tedious and boring. Halfway through my studies, I changed course and joined the Faculty of Arts, tempted by the renowned quality of the professors.

*Me (bottom right) and my friend Fattuma at the campus of
the American University of Beirut (AUB) (1966)*

It was then I realized that Plan B can be just as attractive as Plan A. This is a piece of wisdom that I have since fully embraced in my career and life: Plan and prepare for Plan B to the same extent you strive for what you originally thought; it will prepare you better for the future. More often than not, an alternate goal can be just as rewarding and fulfilling as your original one, filling you with a sense of purpose and meaning as you strive for it.

My switch to the world of social sciences quickly bore fruit, as the professors were masters in their fields, people of intellect and integrity, and beacons of knowledge who left imprints on society then and for years to come. History was being written at AUB, and many of the people who attended, graduated from, or taught at the university during that time period would find themselves in positions of power and influence in their respective countries. Constantine Zurayk, Hanna Batatu, Hisham Sharabi, Fayez Sayegh, Elie Salem, and Walid Khalidi were political forces of nature. It was quite impressive to see Batatu correct information in a textbook about Communism in Sudan, or Khalidi dress down in fluent English an American student for a lack of logic in a presentation. Outside of the classroom, campus life was vibrant, intellectually stimulating, filling me with a passion I had not previously found. I still remember listening to poetry from a Soviet dissident, Aleksandr Solzhenitsyn, and the enchanting musical performance by Ravi Shankar at the chapel. Here I felt at home for the remainder of my undergraduate years.

I have only vague memories of my 1968 commencement ceremony, which my mother attended. As I returned to Kuwait,

I had it in mind to pursue graduate studies. I was certain that I would be granted a scholarship, as Kuwait University had previously announced that all who were accepted for graduate studies would receive one. However, I was forced to rely on yet another Plan B when Kuwait University reversed course and offered no scholarships after all. Convinced that I was destined for a future in academia, I was suddenly at a loss for what to do with my life, a perennial problem to which I am certain many young people can relate. My eventual switch to the diplomatic service was as fortuitous as it was unexpected; a relative who was then the Kuwaiti Undersecretary of the Ministry of Foreign Affairs paid my mother a visit with his wife, and he suggested I look into the diplomatic service. Plan B was a go.

Left to right: Mother, me, and my friend Naila at college graduation, Beirut, Lebanon (1968)

Joining me at the Ministry were two colleagues faced with the same predicament as I when Kuwait University reneged on its offer of graduate scholarships. Our shared, unexpected changes in career and life paths fostered a sense of camaraderie in our office as we took initiatives together. I recall writing a paper with these two colleagues recommending recognition of the People's Republic of China, for example, despite the fact that Kuwait still had diplomatic relations with Taiwan at the time. Our newfound sense of purpose and energy were unfortunately short-lived, as both my colleagues left the Ministry within the year. Prompted in part by the death of my eldest brother, Bader Al Mulla, and also by my disappointment with the Ministry's discriminatory rules against women, I decided it was time for me to leave the diplomatic service as well.

Soon after I made it known that I had opted to embark on my graduate studies but before my last day at the Ministry, I was approached by my boss, Issa Al-Hamad, Director of the Political Department. Sympathizing with my situation, he suggested that I could obtain a scholarship from the Ministry if I agreed to return once I had completed my studies. Knowing the uncertain nature and dearth of opportunities in academia, I eagerly agreed to his proposal and prepared to return to AUB, propelled by my confidence in the professors themselves— their thoroughness, logic, humanity, accomplishments, and gravitas. I wanted to know how their minds worked. Above all, I was drawn to the idea that Walid Khalidi could be my advisor, because I was enamored by the logic of his thoughts. I applied and was accepted into the Political Studies and Public Administration program. Once back in Beirut, I quickly dove into my studies, taking courses not only on politics but also in history and religion.

It was while I was pursuing my graduate studies that I attended an international event for the first time. Prompted by the grace of my boss and mentor Issa Al-Hamad, who was tolerant to my bouts of simmering rebellion against discrimination in the workforce, I attended the United Nations Youth Assembly in 1970 in New York City, an international event that brought together five representatives from each member state of the United Nations.

Me (left) with the other Kuwaiti delegates at the United Nations Youth Assembly (1970)

I can barely even begin to express the sense of awe and wonder that came with being part of such a vibrant and stimulating experience. There were over 640 participants from every corner of the globe, eager to use our young and optimistic minds to solve all the problems of the world. It was chaotic and thrilling, with each and every delegate responsible for their own views rather than those of their respective member states. I felt at home in this environment, surrounded by fellow well-educated, cosmopolitan youths, and in the presence of accomplished people. As the culminating event, Secretary-General U Thant invited all of the delegates to a reception in the UN Garden. Looking back to that period, I cannot help thinking how fortunate I was to be able to meet so many influential and powerful people. Despite this eye-opening experience, I must confess that the highlight of my trip was when my Lebanese friend Roula and I ended up sitting at a table with the celebrated Greek composer and lyricist Mikis Theodorakis, famed for the Zorba dance, at a restaurant in Greenwich Village. How sophisticated we were, sitting with an actual celebrity! Joining us were some of the cast of the Broadway musical *Hair*, famed for the song medley "Aquarius/Let the Sunshine In," who performed in the General Assembly.

My second experience with an international conference was just as enlightening as the first, despite the fact that I would merely be an observer. My professor Walid Khalidi knew of my burgeoning interest in strategic planning and suggested that I attend a Pugwash International event, to be held in a quaint castle in Duino, Italy. I had never heard of Pugwash, much less the tiny village in Nova Scotia from which the conference gets its name. Attending this gathering in 1971 was an eye-opener for me regarding the existence of activity by civil society and civil institutions in the field of arms control. I had thought such topics were reserved for high-ranking officials alone and was completely unaware that grassroots movements existed to address such big-ticket policies. It was inspiring to see scientists and scholars from both sides of the Iron Curtain working together and discussing world affairs in a transparent manner to promote change in the world. From that point on, it was clear to me that civil institutions have a prominent role to play in arms control, and that civil institutions can impact policy on this matter.

Me (right) with a friend at the UN in New York City (1970)

My friend Roula (right) and me at the UN (1970)

My thesis proposal, which was deemed "presumptuous" by an American AUB professor, served only to light a fire under my determination to pursue this subject. After presenting the first draft, a green one, to my advisor Khalidi, it was suggested that I watch movies on nuclear war and learn to play games of chance. I recall him saying that only when I started to dream of nuclear war would I be ready to write about it. I followed his advice and spent some beautiful stress-free time in Beirut watching movies like *On the Beach*, reading books, and playing chess and Chinese checkers in an attempt to saturate and

11

immerse myself with all the knowledge I would need for this undertaking. A few weeks later, I called my advisor, claiming that I was ready. I'd had "a dream." It was true—I did dream that I was in the midst of a nuclear attack. I failed to mention, however, that the only way out was through a laundry shaft to the basement. Given the green light, I commenced with my novel and, at least in *my* mind, a groundbreaking thesis.

Not much was written on nuclear-free zones, and the entire approach to arms control was practically non-existent at AUB. My introduction to this fascinating and often overlooked topic occurred when I took Professor Khalidi's aptly entitled Arms Control and Non-proliferation graduate course. I credit him for sparking my interest and encouraging me in this subject that I have fully embraced in my career. My thesis was entitled, "The Denuclearization of the Middle East." Was it unique? Perhaps. I certainly appreciated it when Professor Elie Salem, former Minister of Foreign Affairs of Lebanon and on the board to approve my thesis, jokingly offered me Lebanese citizenship. Part of my thesis included a proposed General Assembly Resolution on the topic. (See Annex for text of the proposed draft resolution.) I was proud of tackling this maiden topic though it was quite the work of naïve optimism. I passed the gauntlet, but feeling possessive, I requested that my thesis remain out of the public's grasp. This little request to the AUB library would soon be reversed when, to my surprise, I was approached by my supervisors, who informed me that Egyptian officials were keen to have a look at my thesis. I took this as a compliment. One should add that in 1974, Egypt started to join Iran in presenting a resolution to the General Assembly on the establishment of the nuclear-weapon-free zone in the Middle East.

I did not end up attending my own graduation, as I was expected to be back at the Ministry of Foreign Affairs in Kuwait in early 1973 to begin my career in earnest after finishing my dissertation. I had no qualms about this and in fact was eager to fulfill my agreement, due to my love of politics, and with a sense of duty to my country, which had generously funded my graduate education.

Visiting my former advisor Walid Khalidi at his home in Rhode Island (2002)

*Visiting Walid Khalidi at his home in Boston,
Massachusetts (2021)*

First Steps

God grant me the serenity to accept the things I cannot change, the courage to change the things I can, and the wisdom to know the difference.

—Reinhold Niebuhr

Back in Kuwait, I rejoined the Foreign Ministry with a youthful determination to improve the system from within, while steeling myself for the inevitable discrimination heading my way. I knew this was not going to be an easy journey. Other women in the service were aware of the systemic discrimination as well, and indeed one colleague chose to air her grievances on a public radio show in 1973. I was critical of her approach, as I believed that grievances should be shared and dealt with from within the establishment and not aired publicly.

I was assigned to the African Affairs section within the Political Department. I dove into it headfirst, fascinated by the status of countries under colonial rule, and the vibrant liberation movements across the African continent and elsewhere. During my tenure in this position, I met a number of interesting personalities and political figures. Chief among them was the late Oliver Tambo, a prominent figure in the African National Congress. I must have made an impression because even years later, anytime I ran into my South African colleagues from the ANC, they referred to him as my "boyfriend."

In the late summer of 1973, I was selected among other colleagues to assist the Kuwait Mission to the United Nations in New York City during the General Assembly. It was to be a brief, roughly three-month posting that most countries ascribed to in order to beef up their teams in anticipation of the increased workload during the General Assembly. It was also considered a good training ground for junior diplomats.

Attending my first General Assembly session provided a thrill like no other. As an official delegate representing my country and responsible for agenda items, my assignment was to represent Kuwait in the Third Committee, patronizingly referred to as the "Women's Committee" because of the social, cultural, and humanitarian issues it addressed and because the majority of its delegates were women. I was taken aback by the designation and would have much preferred an assignment to the First Committee dealing with arms control and disarmament, but that was the domain of ambassadors. I had no choice. Being the only woman in the delegation, who better to represent Kuwait on the Third Committee? That said, I have always been wary of attempts to superimpose gender in the political fora. In the midst of challenging circumstances, my option was to be protective of my country's reputation. I learned early on that perceptions matter.

Despite these slight misgivings, I was ecstatic to attend my first session at the United Nations. I attentively set about absorbing every proceeding with as much vigilance as I could muster. I was one of five Kuwaiti officials in the Mission, defending, for all practical purposes, the official government census claiming that women constitute 20% of the workforce. This committee, like others, did not have live coverage, instead relying on printed summaries. I diligently read what was known as the Annotated Agenda, which provides a background on every item on the GA or Committees' agendas. One that stood out to me concerned the apartheid regime in South Africa. India was consumed at the time by the treatment of its nationals in apartheid South Africa and introduced the agenda item on "The Rights of Colored People." I thoroughly enjoyed the worldly atmosphere in the UN session and remained captivated by almost every speech given by delegates. My demeanor was simple to read, and I recall the Soviet representative tapping my shoulder and whispering to me that I should not be so awed by the Belorussian representative's speech, as he delivered the same text every year. It would be quite some time before I took his suggestion to heart.

I continued to cover the Third Committee in subsequent sessions and traveled to New York every year. In 1975 the Committee acquired notoriety by passing a resolution equating Zionism with racism and racial discrimination. It was a simple, single line of text that referred to racism and apartheid in an extensive preamble. The resolution energized the non-aligned

17

countries, who found themselves subject to the wrath of the American delegation. Overnight, the "Women's Committee" became the place to be, with ambassadors and delegates clamoring to join, along with media coverage of a degree normally relegated to the Security Council or General Assembly. The resolution even provided United States Ambassador Daniel Patrick Moynihan with a platform from which to launch his senatorial bid.

One especially memorable factor in this discussion was the American use of the Freedom House Indicators for Democracy, to attempt to name and shame various non-aligned countries supportive of the resolution. This effort was grossly undermined by the fact that apartheid South Africa was listed high on that list. Ever since then, I have been wary of indicators, which are more often than not selected by Western liberal democracies. Who is responsible for these indicators and by what standard is the world being judged? American pressure was not to be taken lightly. One sponsor of the draft tearfully told us that he had to withdraw his country's name from the list of co-sponsors. The resolution made its way to the General Assembly and was adopted, resulting in a lengthy quest by the Israeli side to have it revoked. They finally succeeded in 1991 as a concession for Israel's participation in that year's Madrid Conference. I do not recall any other GA resolutions being retracted in such a manner. The irony of the whole episode was evident in the sway of positions: Countries that initially supported the resolution lent their voice to its revocation. This was a testimony to a changing world with the preeminence of the West, and of the US in particular, following the Gulf War in 1991.

The politicization of the Third Committee afforded me flexibility to begin attending other committees, and I relished the opportunity to switch to the First Committee and focus on disarmament and arms control, normally the purview of ambassadors and experts in the field. I found myself attracted to two delegates who, in my opinion, were "stars." One was Alfonso García Robles, the Mexican delegate who was the pillar behind the Treaty of Tlatelolco, calling for the prohibition of nuclear weapons in Latin America and the Caribbean. The treaty came into force in 1968 and Robles would go on to receive the Nobel Peace Prize in 1982. He was truly a brilliant man who played a key part in the arduous work of making Latin America a nuclear-free zone, but I distinctly recall his monotonous delivery when he spoke. I found myself nodding off more often than not when listening to his speeches! The other star diplomat was Alva Myrdal of Sweden, who shared the Nobel Peace Prize with Robles. I appreciated her presentations and professional demeanor in a committee predominantly composed of men, and there was no risk of my falling asleep when I heard her speak!

In 1977 Bahrain, Egypt, Iran, and Kuwait banded together to draft a resolution in the General Assembly on the establishment of a nuclear-weapon-free zone in the Middle East. This marked one of the earliest attempts, and it was most definitely one of the only times that would involve Iran and Arab states besides Egypt working in tandem prior to the outbreak of the Iranian Revolution in 1978.

It was around this time, two years after joining the Ministry in mid-1975, that I was honored with an invitation from Kuwait

University to be an ex officio member of the Board of Faculty of Arts and Education for a span of two years. There, I recall airing out my view on the importance of original research in proposals for advanced studies. Additionally, I was thrilled to receive a personal letter from His Excellency Ahmed bin Khalifa Al-Suwaidi, the first Minister of Foreign Affairs of the United Arab Emirates, inviting me to speak at a panel in the Foreign Ministry in Abu Dhabi on denuclearization of the Middle East. His letter was touching. (See Annex for this letter.) It seemed that my AUB connections would continue to come to the fore during my career, since apparently the nascent ministry had among its advisers a former professor from AUB who was aware of my graduate dissertation. An added thrill was the opportunity to rub shoulders with the eminent leading intellectual Professor Albert Hourani, who was professor at Oxford University.

From 1973-1977 I continued to support the Mission during the General Assembly sessions, spending four months of the year in New York, and also providing a good deal of assistance while back at headquarters. I continued to argue for equal rights in the workplace, pay equity, and a promotion, but all of my requests were to no avail. Perhaps the experience in the political field was so fulfilling that it led me to complacency.

Late in the summer of 1978, I was surprised when a colleague informed me that my name had come up for inclusion in the Delegation to the United Nations. I was blasé about the news, thinking it was only a temporary assignment—but then he told me that it was to be a permanent assignment due to Kuwait's impending membership in the UN Security Council

1978–1979. Ambassador Abdulla Bishara had proposed that I join the Mission full time. I was shocked, to say the least, and considered this news a breakthrough for women in the Foreign Ministry, which would now have a permanent female representative instead of just a seasonal one. I was summoned to the Foreign Minister's office, that of His Excellency Sheikh Sabah Al-Ahmad Al-Sabah, where I was formally informed of the designation and told to check with my mother.

With the rash, unearned confidence of youth, I replied that my mother would not mind. When he replied, the tone of Sheikh Sabah's voice alerted me to the fact that something was amiss. "I am not asking you, Nabeela," he said. "I want your mother to voice her opinion." With these words, he specifically signaled that permission from the matriarch of the family was necessary, and it quickly dawned on me how well-entrenched some traditions are in Kuwaiti society. This particular convention reflected undercurrents in Kuwaiti society that defy gender categorization by the general public, and my flippant response that "mother would not mind," is forever burned into my psyche.

My mother was appreciative of Sheikh Sabah's approach. She knew I valued the appointment and displayed confidence and faith that I would grow and thrive in New York. She left me with her words of wisdom, saying, "I do not fear for you." Her approval and encouragement were doubtlessly aided by the fact that we had a family friend, Mary, who had recently moved to New York, and multiple members of the Kuwaiti delegation were also known to the family. At times their attention was over-protective and even suffocating, but I understood that we all do what we must for our family and loved ones.

It might be said that I extended this understanding to my work as I strived to do all I could for my country on the global stage. The Security Council became my raison d'être at the time, as I brushed shoulders with influential people in the highest international decision-making body. One of the non-permanent seats in the Security Council is customarily reserved for Arab countries from the Asian or African groups. While the larger more influential powers such as Japan and India rotated in more frequently, this was Kuwait's first foray into the Security Council, a position we would not hold again until 2018–2019.

Ambassador Abdullah Bishara, Permanent Representative of the State of Kuwait to the United Nations (center), and me (behind him) at the United Nations in New York (1978)

Our first tenure on the Security Council is well-documented in a book by Ambassador Abdullah Bishara, Permanent Representative of the State of Kuwait to the United
Nations, *Two Years in the Security Council,* and it's fair to say
that it was a much different experience from the General
Assembly; we were now in the big leagues, so to speak. The
Five Permanent Members (China, France, the USSR, the
United Kingdom, and the United States) loomed over every
decision and initiative we had to make; it was an achievement
to convince them to join one's side on a given issue, or even
to neutralize their objections. Years later when I was in South
Africa, I would learn of the big five animals—the lion, leopard,
rhino, elephant, and buffalo—and assign each in my mind to
the five permanent Security Council Members.

The first regional challenge that Kuwait, and I by exten-
sion, had to deal with was the 1978 Israeli invasion of Lebanon
and the establishment of the United Nations Interim Force
in Lebanon (UNIFIL), which although originally slated
as an interim force, is present in Southern Lebanon to this
day and has at times taken on an expanded role. Both these
subjects have been well documented by the Lebanese Ambassador at the time, Ghassan Tueni. Since Kuwait was the Arab
country on the Security Council in 1978, Ambassador Bishara
was approached by the then UN Undersecretary-General
for Special Political Affairs, Sir Brian Urquhart. The latter
informed Bishara that the seemingly dormant United Nations
Truce Supervision Organization (UNTSO), a UN observation
mission that had existed since the Arab–Israeli War of 1948,
had monitored the massive incursion by Israel into Lebanon

before it became public knowledge. Subsequent deliberations on UNIFIL included negotiating its mandate. The first draft, favored by Lebanon, included reference to monitoring movement across the border in order to control Palestinian incursions from Lebanon into Israel. Representatives of the Palestinian Liberation Organization were adamantly opposed to any language that would limit control of its movements. The resolution made it through, despite objections from all sides, and the subsequent renewal of the mandate had to withstand repeated attempts by the United States to impose American whims, which included the withholding of the US contribution to UNIFIL. US Ambassador Jean Kirkpatrick also toyed with the idea to delete reference to the "internationally recognized boundary," between Israel and Lebanon. That did not fly.

These were lonely and difficult times in which one had to balance the interests of various parties. This was before the Arabic language was recognized as an official working language of the United Nations, and the mode of communication was an ancient cypher machine, or, if we were lucky, a fax, which posed challenges in our efforts to maintain close contact with officials back home. Despite how much I enjoyed the work I was doing, Western colleagues who wished to consult with the Kuwaiti delegation sometimes balked at discussing policy with a mere attaché. One such instance occurred during a discussion on renewing the United Nations Peacekeeping Force in Cyprus (UNFICYP). I was delegated to meet with my colleagues to discuss this development, only to find out that the meeting was canceled because my job title meant that I was "not viewed as serious enough to warrant the discussion." When I voiced my frustration, I received assurances that my presence was of importance. Though by no means happy with the status quo, I tolerated it, due to how much I enjoyed my exposure to decision-making at the highest level and watching at close range the unfolding of world events.

Another challenge that non-aligned members faced on the Security Council unfolded during attempts to resolve question around the status of Namibia, which had been under South African occupation since the end of World War I. Following the passage of SC Resolution 435 (1978), which put forth proposals for a ceasefire and UN-supervised elections in Namibia, we were hopeful that another vestige of colonialism would finally end. Soon enough our hopes were dashed by intransigent apartheid South Africa and Western powers' resistance to putting pressure on its leadership to move forward with the resolution. It was not until March 1990 that the political process came into fruition and Namibia gained its independence. At the time, I was still in the UN and was disappointed that I was not included in the Kuwaiti delegation to celebrate Namibia's independence. Little did I know that I would be named as Ambassador of Kuwait to Namibia at a later stage of my career.

The events unfolding in southwest Africa were mirrored in other parts of Southern Africa. There were quite a few Security Council resolutions in 1979 that reaffirmed the right of self-determination and national independence of the people of Zimbabwe, all while denouncing the illegal racist regime of Southern Rhodesia that was preventing any progress. US Ambassador Andrew Young was sympathetic to African states' progress toward post-colonial independence and was energetic with his interventions. At one time during these discussions, a British colleague pointed his finger at me while I was working with the non-aligned group and admonished me for failing to support the independence of Southern Rhodesia. He wanted to rush through Security Council procedures without regard to the cautious attitude of the non-aligned countries towards the Rhodesian peace settlement. This was typical of colonial powers, believing they knew what was best with little concern to the consensus of the majority of the international community. As was the case with Namibia, little did I know that I would one day be named Kuwait's Ambassador to Zimbabwe.

Another fascinating but also frustrating issue was Kuwait's attempt to resolve the Chinese incursion into Vietnam in February 1979—ostensibly to punish Vietnam for its own incursion into Cambodia. This issue was our responsibility to address, as Kuwait assumed the presidency of the Security Council in February. A request for an audience at the UN with the Chinese delegation was dismissed due to bad weather. Eventually, we did meet with them, and I was shocked by the response of the representative who slapped his face repeatedly and commented that China just wanted to "teach Vietnam a lesson."

Naturally, resolving the Palestinian question was a priority issue for the Arab States, in and outside of the Security Council. The Palestinians had been trying to push through a resolution; however, they were running into resistance from the American administration, which was under federal instruction not to have meetings with Palestinian representatives. Ambassador

Abdullah Bishara arranged for an informal encounter between Ambassador Andrew Young and the Palestinian Liberation Organization Ambassador Zuhdi Tarazi at the Kuwaiti ambassador's residence, which I only learned about when he handed me a script of the encounter and asked me to rewrite, seal, and send it to our Foreign Minister. I initially demurred, wanting instead to keep following the ongoing discussion in the Security Council; however, I quickly relented. In the privacy of my office, I read the letter of the encounter with awe. Nothing came from this meeting, and Ambassador Young resigned shortly after, ostensibly due to his disagreement with the US Administration. The meeting eventually became public knowledge.

Turbulent Times

*Kuwait's membership in the UN is not an end by itself
but a way of participating in the responsibility for a
better life or its own people and peoples of the world.*

—Sheikh Sabah Al-Ahmed Al-Sabah

The period between the departure of Ambassador Bishara and the arrival of the new Ambassador Mohammed Abul-hassan coincided with the outbreak of the Iran–Iraq War in September 1980. During this time, Kuwait held the presidency of the League of Arab States (LAS) and was entrusted to present the Arab view at the UN Security Council.

All of our energy was poured into monitoring and working to resolve this conflict. As an Arab country, Kuwait was expected to fall in line with the general sympathetic sentiment in support of Iraq. As the war broadened in scope and size, we increasingly overlooked or marginalized other international and regional issues at the United Nations. The Iraqi delegation went so far as to distribute talking points and elicited compliance from Arab delegations, which I personally considered to be high-handed of them. Indeed, on one occasion I recall that President Saddam Hussein hardly negotiated with the rest of the Arab group, instead dictating what he wanted to hear. Kuwait attempted to mediate on the international stage through the Gulf Cooperation Council (GCC), League of Arab States, or the Organization of Islamic Conference in order to find a solution to the conflict. Throughout the war, however, President Hussein never accepted mediation efforts; he only expected allegiance.

For the first couple of years, the Iran–Iraq War remained relatively contained as a protracted conflict between the two states. In 1984, as the stalemate dragged on, Iraq escalated the fight by conducting attacks on Iranian oil tankers in the Gulf. Iran retaliated by conducting their own strikes on Kuwaiti and Saudi tankers. This spurred the international community to come together and pass SC Resolution 552 (1984) calling for and affirming the right of free navigation in international waters and shipping lanes. The resolution did not include any method of enforcement, and it was soon forgotten, due to this omission and the fact that the attacks were more of a nuisance than a serious threat.

In 1986, however, Iran stepped up its attacks and began singling out Kuwaiti tankers. We approached both the Soviet Union and the United States with the goal of reflagging our tankers in order to ensure their protection. Given the security situation, the Soviets and the Americans were amenable to the request. We opted to rely more heavily on the Americans but nevertheless leased a few Soviet ships as well. This arrangement earned the ire of the delegation of the People's Democratic Republic of Yemen (South Yemen), which expressed to us their opposition to any agreement that would increase the influence of the United States in the region. Less than a decade later, the Gulf would once again be at the center of the international stage when the international community engaged in a naval blockade of Iraq to enforce the sanctions mandated by SC Resolution 665 (1990) following Iraq's invasion of Kuwait. As those events unfolded, I remember musing at the strategic importance and international nature of this relatively small waterway.

Rather early into the Iraq–Iran war, on 7 June 1981, the Israeli Air Force conducted a surprise airstrike and destroyed the unfinished Osirak nuclear reactor near Baghdad. This attack was met with intense criticism of Israel by the international community and led to their censure in two separate resolutions in the Security Council and General Assembly. It was the first time, in my recollection, that the Security Council passed a resolution calling for Israel to submit its nuclear facilities to IAEA safeguards.

War weariness and the military stalemate, coupled with the rising human and economic costs of the war, convinced the Iranians to "drink the poison" and agree to a ceasefire based on SC Resolution 598 (1988). Part of the resolution included a return to the "internationally recognized boundary," a statement referring to the 1975 Algiers Agreement, abrogated by Saddam Hussein prior to the start of the conflict. It also requested the Secretary-General to explore, in consultation with Iran and Iraq, the question of entrusting an impartial body with an inquiry into responsibility for the conflict and to report to the Council as soon as possible. Furthermore, it implored the Secretary-General to examine, in consultation with Iran and Iraq and with other states of the region, measures to enhance security and stability.

The paragraph encouraging measures to enhance the security and stability of the region seemed vague and inconsequential. I never gave it more than the attention I thought it merited, until my Russian and Iranian colleagues began referencing it when addressing a security arrangement within the Gulf. During a 2004 courtesy call to Ambassador Sergey Lavrov, for example, he explicitly made reference to SC Resolution 598 (1988) when discussing security concerns in the Gulf with me.

It was not until December 1991 that UN Secretary-General Javier Pérez de Cuellar wrote a letter to the Security Council in which he outlined that Iraq had engaged in the "illegal use of force and the disregard for the territorial integrity of a UN member state"[1] For the Iranians, this was a victory and an exoneration, since many countries had been sympathetic to the Iraqis. However, the report received little fanfare, and the international reaction was subdued, most likely due to the United Nations' focus on resolving pending issues following the liberation of Kuwait.

Due in part to our own experience of vulnerability, Kuwait has played a significant role in the realm of international peacekeeping. The aforementioned United Nations Interim Force in

---

1 S/23273 of 9 December 1991

Lebanon (UNIFIL) is a prime example of Kuwait's commitment and support for such efforts. We not only assisted with
the drafting of the mandate establishing the force, but also navigated through its financial difficulties, such as the withholding
of financial contributions by the United States. Throughout,
Kuwait's dedication remained unwavering, with contributions
amounting to 0.233% of the force's budget and totaling $15.2
million.

Moving forward, Kuwait continued its active involvement in peacekeeping initiatives, exemplified by its support
for the United Nations Iran–Iraq Military Observer Group
(UNIIMOG) from 1988 to February 1991. In this case,
Kuwait's commitment extended beyond financial contributions, as the country donated vehicles to kickstart the mission.
However, a twist in the narrative unfolded when Iraq claimed
these vehicles as its own contribution to the United Nations,
revealing the complexities of facts on the ground.

Kuwait naturally was engaged with the United Nations
Iraq-Kuwait Observation Mission (UNIKOM) from April
1991 to 2003. During this period, UNIKOM underwent a
transformation in its mandate, evolving from a mere observer
group to a force capable of using military power when necessary. Notably, this mission marked one of the first times that
all five permanent members of the United Nations Security
Council participated jointly in a peacekeeping mission. Kuwait
took on a substantial financial burden, covering two-thirds
of UNIKOM's budget. In navigating discussions about the
possibility of Kuwait shouldering the full cost, we argued for
the equitable distribution of financial responsibilities among

member states, emphasizing the necessity of a shared international commitment.

Finally, Kuwait also participated in the United Task Force (UNITAF) in Somalia, which set a precedent for the country's involvement in international peacekeeping endeavors. Notably, this mission was characterized by its humanitarian focus, showcasing Kuwait's contribution to global peace and stability.

The Gulf War and Its Aftermath

People rarely win wars; governments rarely lose them.
—Arundhati Roy

Throughout the years I worked at Kuwait's Ministry of Foreign Affairs, I kept raising the issue of equalizing my salary and status with those of my colleagues. Prompted by the knowledge that a local employee at the Mission in New York had preferential pay over me, in 1989 I decided it was time for me to make a bold stand by putting my grievance in writing and personally handing it to the Foreign Minister. Opportunity arose before I could do so, however, when I received an impromptu invitation to state my case before Sheikh Sabah. He granted his immediate approval to change my status from administrative staff to full-fledged diplomatic staff. Although it seemed my seniority was not exactly taken into consideration, I recall being taken aback at the ease with which he made his decision. It was amazing to think that my livelihood and career prospects could be so simply approved.

By the end of the Iran-Iraq war, I had been at the United Nations for over eleven consecutive years. I began experiencing what colleagues and I referred to as "UN fatigue," and in the spring of 1990, I expressed the wish to move on. My position as the first woman diplomat perhaps lent special credence, however, and I was told to wait until September. Iraq's invasion of Kuwait on 2 August 1990 ensured my tenure at the UN would last a little longer. Indeed all diplomatic operations continued; however, there was no possibility of staff relocation during that time.

Throughout the Iran-Iraq War and the 1990 invasion of Kuwait, I had taken a special interest in Iraq and diligently followed any news or announcements regarding the Middle East region. I was a keen follower of the pricey *Foreign Broadcast Information Service* (FBIS), which, much to the chagrin of my administrative colleagues, was published by the US government. The confidence of the Iraqi leadership was apparent as their aspiration to lead the region—and indeed the entire developing world—became more pronounced. Meanwhile, Egypt, for decades the political and military leader of the Arab world, was marginalized following its decision to make peace with Israel in 1979, and Iran had made itself a pariah on the international stage due to its contentious policies following its 1979 revolution. Additionally, the perceived power vacuum resulting from waning Soviet influence and a rudderless

Non-Aligned Movement called for the emergence of strong leadership. Saddam Hussein seemed to believe that he, and Iraq, would assume this mantle.

Strapped for cash and facing a slew of domestic problems and infrastructure failures in the summer of 1990, an emboldened Iraq turned its attention to the Gulf countries. Kuwait and the United Arab Emirates (UAE) were clearly Hussein's favored targets, with allegations that depreciating oil prices and thus the shrinking Iraqi economy were a result of overproduction by both Gulf states. At an OPEC meeting in July, Iraq threatened the use of force to ensure implementation of an oil quota, and its defiant tone and persistent posturing forced Kuwait to delay our oil team's planned maiden visit to Namibia. Iraq was presumably emboldened by the words of April Glaspie, the US Ambassador to Iraq at the time, that the US "[has] no opinion on the Arab-Arab conflicts, like your border disagreement with Kuwait," and an earlier communication from the US State Department to Hussein stating that Washington had "no special defense or security commitments to Kuwait."[2] Ambassador Glaspie added that she was concerned about Iraq's massive troop deployment on the Kuwaiti border while the Iraqi government branded Kuwait's actions in the oil industry as "parallel to military aggression." Such a stance seemed to be the acceptable American position on border disputes between states. Years later Secretary of State Hillary Clinton would echo Glaspie's words when asked to comment on a dispute between

---

2 www.nytimes.com/1990/09/23/world/confrontation-in-the-gulf-us-gave-iraq-little-reason-not-to-mount-kuwait-assault.html

China and Japan in the South China Sea.[3]

I took a break to visit family in London, where they usually spent summer holidays, before returning to New York that uncertain year. At a reception at the UN, a friend took me by the arm, howling, "Why don't you seek American assistance?!" Towing the official line, I expressed confidence in mediation and spoke of avoiding the possibility of intimidating Iraq. Placing my faith in the mediators and diplomats currently in Jeddah, I resumed my leave and departed for Long Island with a lighter heart.

That feeling would not last. I learned of the invasion from Ted Koppel when I turned on the television to watch *Nightline* on 2 August 1990. His words, "…and we shall keep you informed about the invasion of Kuwait," stunned me. My first impulse was to call home, but I could not get through. I called the Mission on my old-fashioned car phone and stayed on the line through the entire time I sped back to Manhattan.

The Security Council was abuzz at midnight following a request by Kuwait, as well as requests from the US and UK, for an immediate meeting. It was during those first official deliberations of the Security Council on what would become known as SC Resolution 660 (1990) that the American Permanent Representative, Thomas Pickering, announced in the public session that Kuwait's ruling family had crossed into Saudi Arabia and was safe. Our delegation had no clue of that development at the time and were much relieved!

Meanwhile, private consultations among the members of

---

3 https://www.voanews.com/a/clinton-urges-asean-china-to-agree-maritime-conduct-code/1500695.html

the Security Council were delayed until the Yemeni Ambassador was located, and they concentrated on the text of the
resolution. An Ethiopian colleague advised me to compile a
sheet of news from the wires and make it available to the other
delegations, which proved to be an invaluable tool in garnering
support for our assertion of Iraq's immediate withdrawal from
Kuwait. Yemen argued for a ceasefire, but the phrase "immediate withdrawal" would triumph in the end for the simple
fact that there was no ongoing military confrontation; it was a
brazen invasion.

This final wording came to be when the Yemenis relented,
as the UAE persuaded them not to participate in the vote, in
lieu of abstaining, since non-participation is perceived as a
less hostile stance than abstention. China had popularized
this mode of action, which other countries would often utilize
when wishing to confer vagueness on an official position. The
international community's overwhelming support of SC Resolution 660 (1990) was as impressive as it was touching, and
it included some truly remarkable shows of solidarity. For
example, as I walked back to the office in the early hours of the
morning after the resolution's passage, worn out by our overnight negotiations, an Iranian delegate rushed to my side. He
informed me that upon his return to New York, Ambassador
Mohammad Javad Zarif would convey the message that Iran
would lend its support to Kuwait. That news certainly lifted
my mood. What a change from the time when Kuwait was
supporting Iraq in its war against Iran!

That same day, I also received a voicemail from the Secretary-General of the Organization of African Unity (OAU),

Salim Ahmed Salim, inquiring about the safety of His Highness the Amir Sheikh Jaber Al-Ahmad Al-Sabah and the rest of the ruling family. He had left this message before the announcement was made of the family's safe passage into Saudi Arabia, and as I sat on the edge of my bed and listened to his voice asking if he could be of any assistance, I broke down sobbing. I called him back and suggested that an OAU statement demanding complete withdrawal would be the best approach, given that the League of Arab States was still deliberating the issue in Cairo. The OAU statement followed shortly thereafter, echoing the Security Council Resolution.

The passage of the resolution went unheeded by Iraq. During the early period of the occupation, His Highness the Amir Sheikh Jaber Al-Ahmad Al-Sabah sent individual letters to over thirty heads of state, invoking Article 51 of the UN Charter, inviting them to lend assistance to Kuwait in repelling the occupation. Our delegation was entrusted with transmitting a number of these letters, due to the fact that Kuwait did not have embassies in a number of countries. The United States would also use this opportunity to invoke Article 51 of the Charter to legitimize sending troops to the region. And ultimately, the adoption of SC Resolution 660 (1990) in the early hours of the morning was followed by similar ordeals of overnight negotiations throughout the next six months. Working for 48-hour stretches was common for all of us in the delegation, and in a way, the pace numbed personal emotions. We were too tired and too focused to expend our energies on anger or anxiety.

It was at this time, between 2–6 August 1990, that the

USSR and the United States took the unusual step of jointly appealing to the international community to halt all arms deliveries to Iraq. This appeal preceded SC Resolution 661 (1990) on 6 August, imposing sanctions.

Another noteworthy resolution in the group that followed was SC Resolution 662 (1990) on 9 August, which was presented by the six Gulf Cooperation Council states against Iraq's "comprehensive and eternal merger," with Kuwait. It was adopted unanimously and coincided, ironically, with Saddam Hussein's offer to achieve full peace with Iran, recognizing the pre-war borders and withdrawing its troops. Whether he meant this as a genuine gesture of peace, or as a bargaining tool to further his own goals in Kuwait by freeing soldiers tied up in Iran and circumventing sanctions, is a matter of debate. When a media friend who had avoided me during the first few days of the invasion finally asked my opinion on the matter, I replied that if Hussein were to secure a long coastline, which he did after annexing Kuwait, there would be no need to cross swords with Iran over their shared border.

One could not say that the occupation period constituted "business as usual"; however, Kuwait did keep up its presence on the international stage. A particular instance that really raised eyebrows occurred when Sheikh Sabah Al-Ahmad Al-Sabah participated in Palestinian Solidarity Day. Perceptions at the time were that Kuwait would turn its back on the Palestinian cause, given the PLO's support of Saddam Hussein. We also endeavored to be present at academic events outside the United Nations whenever we were invited. Misinformation and manipulation of public opinion was pervasive. I recall that in a discussion at the University of Maryland, a participant claimed that the US administration had intentionally selected 15 January 1991 to implement Security Council resolutions to coincide with Martin Luther King, Jr. Day. In fact, the French and Russians had recommended adding a date in order to avoid leaving the issue open-ended.

If there is one thing I learned during my career as a diplomat, it is that sensible arguments and good personal relations can have an impact on people, and I cultivated positive relations with a broad cross-section of public figures and people in the media. I recall reaching out to a CNN correspondent based at the UN to say that it was painful to see reporting on the occupation of Kuwait while UN personnel were lowering the Kuwaiti flag in the background. It is a normal occurrence to raise and lower the UN flags every day; however, this televised sight added an unnecessary extra layer of hurt. The importance of a flag as a symbol of national pride cannot be underestimated. Kuwait waited two years after independence to raise its flag on UN grounds after its application to the United Nation was officially recognized. The CNN correspondent was understanding of my point, and such insensitive filming was not repeated. I thought of this exchange in late September 2015, when I related the incident of Kuwait's flag raising at the UN to the powerful and emotional moment when President Mahmoud Abbas raised the Palestinian flag there for the first time.

Another issue I attended to in the aftermath of the adoption of SC Resolution 662 (1990) was the perennial resolution presented by Iraq to the General Assembly on the security and safety of nuclear installations. This was intended as a follow-up to their successful passing of SC Resolution 487 (1981) after the Israeli raid on Iraq's Osirak nuclear reactor. Notwithstanding whether we agreed with the text of the resolution in principle, Kuwait was of the opinion that Iraq should be denied credibility on the world stage. A "friendly" colleague from Libya attempted to dissuade us from presenting amendments which would have rendered the Iraqi draft resolution obsolete, to no avail. Kuwait decided to go it alone, without a co-sponsorship of Western and other delegations. I recall presenting the phrase, "...condemning the placement of people as human shields at strategic sites," among others, when trying to torpedo the Iraqi diplomatic initiative.

In all, twelve resolutions were passed between 2 August and 29 November 1990 when SC Resolution 678 (1990) finally authorized member states to use "all necessary means" to force Iraq out of Kuwait by a deadline of 15 January 1991. To those unfamiliar with the inner workings of pushing through Security Council resolutions, I state unequivocally that the passage of 678 was nothing short of miraculous, a marvelous feat of tireless behind-the-scenes diplomatic efforts. Indeed, a Serbian colleague at the time commented that while he was sympathetic to our cause, he lamented that Kuwait was getting attention when Yugoslavia, in the midst of its messy breakup, was all but marginalized. It was only the third time that the Security Council would authorize the use of armed force against another state, and the first time with the support of all permanent members. The first authorization of force was in 1950 during the Korean crisis, to pressure North Korea to withdraw from the south. In that instance, it only passed due to a Soviet boycott of the Security Council meeting, since China's seat was, at the time, occupied by Taiwan. The second time was authorizing the United Kingdom to enforce sanctions in South Rhodesia by way of a naval blockade.

All of our weekends leading up to the passage of Resolution 678 were consumed with negotiations, meetings, and receptions, with everyone at the Mission giving up our free time so that any venue for championing Kuwait's cause was attended to. The line between vanity and presentability was heavily blurred during that time period. "You look terrible." These were the first words I heard from a friend during the one rare instance when I had a few hours off.

We wanted to be involved in the discussions, resolutions, and decision-making during the occupation of Kuwait; however, there were some instances where our input was not sought. A case in point: We were not even aware of certain diplomatic moves, such as when the French spearheaded issues around besieged diplomats who were still in Kuwait. When I finally heard about their efforts, I was taken aback by our exclusion. In this and other similar cases, it became clear that individual states' interests were taking precedence over the occupation of Kuwait! This sobering realization forced all of us at the Mission to be savvy in our reliance on personal contacts to inform us of any change in the winds. For example, during negotiations around one of the many resolutions concerning the occupation, I reached out to Ambassador Amara Essy of Côte d'Ivoire, who was a good friend of mine, largely due to introductions through a mutual friend, Boubaker Adjali, a veteran of the National Liberation Front and an accomplished media man in Algeria, Africa, and at the UN. In fact, Adjali was the go-between who requested that I secure passage for Amara and other colleagues to Mecca a few years back, since Côte d'Ivoire had no relations with Saudi Arabia. In 1990 Côte d'Ivoire was a non-permanent member of the UNSC. Amara was not in New York at the time, and since generally resolutions are much better received publicly and officially if their co-sponsors are from different regions and include non-permanent members, I sent him a personal message requesting that Côte d'Ivoire co-sponsor a draft resolution. On the day of the Security Council meeting to consider the resolution, his deputy had no instructions from the capital, but before the meeting started he left the chamber. Ten minutes later he returned and announced that Côte d'Ivoire would co-sponsor the resolution. The importance of personal relationships cannot be overstated!

With SC Resolution 678 (1990) adopted in late November and nicknamed the "enabling resolution," liberation became a realistic goal. In the meantime, Iraq's occupation continued to wreak havoc in Kuwait as the 15 January 1991 deadline for Iraqi withdrawal loomed. In early December 1990, Iraq placed explosives on the Kuwaiti oil wells, eventually setting around 700 of them on fire. It was an unprecedented ecological disaster. In response, a Finnish colleague approached me with a proposal to resurrect an obscure legal instrument aimed at deterring military action with ecological repercussions. Concerns were raised that this might not go well with our allies, as it would bring to the fore military actions elsewhere that impacted the environment, so although I appreciated my Finnish colleague's ingenuity, we did not end up pursuing this idea.

At the outset of the fires, Kuwait was advised by American expert Red Adair, who stated that extinguishing the oil wells would be a two-year endeavor. Undaunted, Kuwait enlisted a wide number of teams from over 15 countries, including Iran, Canada, Poland, and Hungary, the latter being renowned for using jet turbines to extinguish fires. Notably, Kuwait participated in this fire-fighting mission with the only woman, Sara Akbar, among the whole lot. Contrary to the earlier dire expectations, the roughly 700 oil-well fires were extinguished less than a year after they began, on 6 November 1991.

There was an interest at the time in pursuing the Iraqi regime for crimes against Kuwait in order to exact some criminal justice through an international court system. This avenue was never pursued in earnest, and retribution was exacted through a compensation commission and sanctions. The experience did, however, inspire Kuwait to introduce a resolution in the General Assembly in 2001 to designate 6 November as World Environment Day. The resolution, which was adopted by consensus, called for the safeguarding of the environment during wartime and military confrontation.

As a testament to the trials endured in the harrowing days of Iraqi occupation, I kept and framed the front page of *The New York Times Magazine* featuring a photograph captured by the world-renowned Brazilian photographer Sebastião Salgado of the oil fires raging in Kuwait. I brought this framed piece with me through my various postings as a constant and physical reminder of the Iraqi occupation, and it remains in my office to this day.

The fires of Kuwait captured by my brother, Anwar, in April 1991

While the oil-well fires were still raging in early 1991, the international community prepared for war, anticipating Iraq's failure to withdraw from Kuwait. United States Chairman of the Joint Chiefs of Staff Colin Powell commented on the emergence of a strong coalition, describing it "a smooth one" and "a dream of all operations." However, as the coalition gathered in Saudi Arabia, ready to commence operations, sympathy from some developing countries began to wane. Many were distrustful of the US, and anti-Americanism was rampant. A Cuban colleague, for example, took pains to assure me that mistrust of the United States' policies, rather than any sentiments against Kuwait, had led them to vote against SC Resolution 678 and its 15 January 1991 deadline for Iraqi withdrawal.

Iraq, of course, failed to meet this deadline. When utilizing "all necessary means," the coalition was responsible for notifying the Security Council of any action taken in implementing the resolutions, and on the eve of the operation to evict Iraq, our delegation made sure that Kuwait's letter of notification preceded that of the allies. Then, during the course of the coalition's military operation, Kuwait went on the diplomatic offensive by sending envoys to several countries in defense of the use of force to liberate the country. These envoys were assisted by diplomatic staff from our Mission at the UN. I joined the Minister of Higher Education, Ali Al-Shamlan, and his deputy on visits to Cuba, Venezuela, and Argentina.

Our meeting with President Fidel Castro was quite memorable. We boarded a private flight from Miami, hoping to return the same day after making our presentation. We ended up having to wait until late in the night to meet with the President. When Minister Al-Shamlan began his presentation, Castro interrupted him to share his thoughts on the outbreak of cholera in Peru. His inattentiveness to our presentation and sudden change of subject was a bit shocking, but at least he did not launch into a tirade about the American-led coalition war effort. Our meeting with Argentinian President Carlos Menem went more smoothly. At the time, Kuwait had no diplomatic representation in Argentina, and so the Saudi Ambassador took care of all the logistics of our visit. As President Menem was of Syrian origin, we presented him with tapes of Arabic hymns at a Syrian church. He invited us to explore Argentina's legendary tourist sites, but we were in no position or mood to honor the offer. After our meetings there, I left the delegation and returned directly to New York upon the request of my Ambassador.

The liberation of Kuwait and victory over Iraq occurred on 26 February, and I was eager for a homecoming. Before I took off, I still had some duties to attend to. Coincidentally, it fell on me as charge d'affaires to transmit a letter from the Deputy Prime Minister and Minister of Foreign Affairs notifying the Secretary-General of the return of the legitimate government to the country. The government had taken up exile in Taif, Saudi Arabia during the occupation.

Nabeela Al Mulla

Security Council

Distr.
GENERAL

S/22338
6 March 1991

ORIGINAL: ENGLISH

LETTER DATED 6 MARCH 1991 FROM THE CHARGE D'AFFAIRES A.I. OF THE
PERMANENT MISSION OF KUWAIT TO THE UNITED NATIONS ADDRESSED TO
THE SECRETARY-GENERAL

I have the honour to transmit herewith a message from His Excellency
Sheikh Sabah Al-Ahmad Al-Jaber Al Sabah, Deputy Prime Minister and Minister of
Foreign Affairs, addressed to Your Excellency.

I should appreciate it if you would arrange for this message to be circulated
as a document of the Security Council.

(Signed) Nabeela AL-MULLA
Chargé d'affaires a.i.

Annex

[Original: Arabic/English]

Letter dated 4 March 1991 from the Deputy Prime Minister
and Minister for Foreign Affairs of Kuwait addressed to
the Secretary-General

I have the honour and pleasure to inform you that the Government of Kuwait is
resuming the functions of the State and directing the affairs of the nation from
Kuwait City.

I should like to seize this opportunity to express our gratitude and
appreciation to you personally and to the United Nations system as a whole for the
indispensable role played to reverse the Iraqi aggression and to end the occupation
of Kuwait.

The contribution of the United Nations system to the restoration of Kuwait's
territorial integrity, and the return of the legitimate government to the country
has reconfirmed the purposes and objectives of the Charter and the importance of
the Organization in maintaining international peace and security.

Sabah Al-Ahmad Al-Jaber AL SABAH
Deputy Prime Minister
and Minister of Foreign Affairs

*Letter from the Deputy Prime Minister and Minister of Foreign Affairs of
Kuwait to the Secretary-General stating that the Kuwaiti Government is
resuming the functions of the State, 6 March 1991. (UN Digital Library)*

It was a time of chaos and uncertainty, with the people and the government of Kuwait striving to return to a sense of normalcy. The burning oil wells blackened the sky and by some reports even caused "black snow" to fall as far as Nepal. I was tasked with taking 32 items, such as satellite telephones, antennas, and the like, to Kuwait for the government, a job that initially seemed impossible, since a number of airlines balked at the size of my luggage. I had to wait an extra day for Kuwait's national airline to resume operations, and then I flew from New York to London to Manama, Bahrain, where I was told I would have to wait until the winds changed course so that we would have an opportunity to land. When a window opened up, I rushed to the airport to board an official government flight, eager to finally go home.

While I had heard of the fires, nothing could have prepared me, or anyone on my flight, for what we witnessed as we flew into Kuwait. The roar of the fires seemed to reverberate in my skull, the angry black smoke looking like a venomous serpent slithering up into the sky. The entire plane was silent; we were all in shock. After landing and my quick debriefing, the government arranged transportation for me to visit my family. It is difficult to describe how I felt, pulling up to my family's home in a suburb of Kuwait City–it was as if my heart felt lighter and heavier all at the same time. Immediately I was struck by the presence of iron bars all around the windows and doors of the first floor. That was new. I banged on the door, only to be immediately rebuffed. I banged again and was rewarded with annoyed and flabbergasted looks on my sisters' faces, which rapidly turned to joy. Needless to say, it was an emotional reunion. There were too many stories to be told in too short a time; duty ever calls, and I was instructed to remain on call for an opening to fly back to New York and return to my duties.

The Security Council passed SC Resolution 687 (1991) for the peace terms, which included the demarcation of the boundary between Kuwait and Iraq. An Egyptian colleague confided in me that this was the time to resolve this issue with Iraq once and for all. The UNSC established the Iraq-Kuwait Boundary Demarcation Commission, which spent the next two years on the ground documenting and delineating the border and waterways. Its membership included professionals from New Zealand, Norway, and Indonesia, in addition to representatives from Iraq and Kuwait. Kuwait decided to take the extra step of sending envoys to several countries with personal letters from the Foreign Minister to shore up support of the demarcation that was ultimately endorsed by the UN. I was then serving as Deputy Chief of the Mission and, together with other Kuwaiti ambassadors, I was invited to a joint meeting in Paris to discuss how to proceed with garnering support for the demarcation process. The Ministry of Foreign Affairs assigned each of us regions to visit, equipped us with letters and maps, and sent us on our way to our respective destinations, which included Asia, Latin America, and Africa. I was personally tasked with delivering these letters to the foreign ministers of Zimbabwe, Botswana, and Zambia.

Lieutenant-General Mohammed Al-Bader (right) with me (next to him) and other UN and Kuwaiti officials at a visit to the Kuwait–Iraq border posts (1993)

With Lieutenant-General Mohammed Al-Bader

I was also entrusted to liaise with the United Nations Department of Peacekeeping Operations on the demarcation of the boundary with Iraq. UN officers on the ground were more forthcoming than officers at headquarters. In fact, Austrian Major-General Gunther Greindl, commander of UNIKOM, gave me his copy of the map when headquarters withheld it. It was an unprecedented feat for UN involvement on a boundary issue between member states. Upon completion of the task and adoption of SC Resolution 833 (1993), the Kuwaiti Lieutenant-General Mohammed Al-Bader was tasked by the government with the supervision of security issues of the border. This included erecting nineteen posts along the whole length of the demarcated border. Together with other Kuwaiti colleagues, I visited the sites.

Security along the border was enforced by UN peacekeepers and patrols by the Kuwait National Guard. I thought the issue was resolved, only to be reminded of the importance of follow-up when I relocated to Southern Africa and accompanied Lieutenant-General Al-Bader on his survey of the border fencing between South Africa and Zimbabwe. That experience prompted me to reframe my perception of the Iraq-Kuwait border demarcation to conclude that it was not resolved but contained. Therefore, it needed to be revisited to be entrenched. Lieutenant-General Al-Bader surveyed other border arrangements, but in the end, Kuwait opted for the South African one because of its feasibility and success.

Moreover, there was the issue of our prisoners of war. Following the end of the Gulf War, there were thousands of Kuwaiti POWs that were unaccounted for. This was addressed in the omnibus SC Resolution 686 (1991), which demanded that Iraq arrange for the release of and immediate access to all POWs under the auspices of the International Committee of the Red Cross (ICRC). In early 1992, while on holiday in Austria, I was instructed to attend a tripartite meeting in Geneva organized by the ICRC to address this issue. Representatives from the US, UK, France, Saudi Arabia, and Kuwait were on one side, with Iraq on the other, and the ICRC chairing as a neutral party. During the meeting, a French diplomat personally confided to me that we should adhere to this international mechanism, noting that the bilateral negotiation between Iraq and Iran regarding their prisoners was progressing very slowly. This mechanism, along with turmoil in southern Iraq following the end of the war, enabled over 6,000 POWs to return home. However, the fate of the remaining 600 was unclear, and to this day, around 300 people are still unaccounted for.

Madrid Conference 1991 and ACRS Participation

As the dust settled after the Gulf War, there was a wave of hope that change could come to other parts of the Middle East. An international initiative by way of the Madrid Conference of 1991 spearheaded by the United States brought optimism that the long-standing Arab-Israeli conflict might finally be resolved. The conference primarily aimed to revive bilateral talks between Israel and its neighbors. Meanwhile, it also commissioned the establishment of five specialized groups, each dedicated to tackling critical aspects of the complex issue. These groups were designed to address the intricate dynamics

of the conflict, focusing on crucial areas such as the environment, water resources, refugees, economic development, and
arms control. Early on, I learned from an American official that
the inclusion of arms control was in direct response to Egypt's
request!

It was during this period that I was tasked to represent
Kuwait in the Arms Control and Regional Security Committee,
more commonly referred to as the ACRS Group. I was unaware
at the time how much my experience in this fledgling group
would prepare me for the challenges that lay ahead in my career.
The initial meeting took place in Washington, DC in May 1992
and delved into a multitude of operational and conceptual
concerns. The agenda encompassed pressing issues, ranging
from forging agreements on robust communication protocols,
to devising comprehensive frameworks for maritime search-
and-rescue operations, and to establishing necessary protocols
for the timely notification of military activities.

The path to progress, however, was not without its challenges. The notable absence of Lebanon and Syria, due to their
complex political entanglements with Israel, presented a significant hurdle in our multilateral approach. Lacking the involvement of these key stakeholders not only hindered substantive
discussion, but also cast a shadow on the prospects of achieving
meaningful breakthroughs in the bilateral track.

During this time, representatives in the Committees from
the GCC countries convened in Riyadh to deliberate and
assess the extent of their participation in the various working
groups. It became increasingly apparent that the slow pace of
progress in addressing the political bilateral issues within the

ACRS Group was dampening Kuwait's resolve to fully commit to the Committee's thrust. I only attended a few meetings between Washington, DC and Moscow before Kuwait decided to tone down its engagement. Apparently the ACRS project became a reference for researchers and politicians to stimulate renewed interest in the idea of a Middle East zone free of weapons of mass destruction. I became aware of this interest twenty years later, when I received an out-of-the-blue call to provide a contribution to the ACRS Oral History project.

I had been at the UN posting for around fourteen years by this point in time, and my colleagues had moved on to higher assignments. I was keen to follow suit. The next phase of my career would take me to Africa, where my first posting as Ambassador was to Zimbabwe and would prove to be a testing ground. As the next chapter details, it was a self-inflicted trial.

Into Africa

It's a lonely place at the top.
—Nabeela Al Mulla

An Historic Post in Zimbabwe

During the ambassadors' meeting in Paris discussing how to garner support for the demarcation process, there was a side discussion with the Undersecretary of the Ministry of Foreign Affairs on several vacancies in ambassadorial posts, which included Zimbabwe. "I would love to go there," I blurted. I remember the flabbergasted look on his face in the silence that followed before he asked, "You want to go from New York to... Zimbabwe?"

It was here that my previous experience working on the African file piqued my interest. Yes, I wanted to go to Zimbabwe, I explained, not only because it was past time that I should be granted my own post as Ambassador, but also because I felt we shouldn't abandon a country or a region just because it was no longer on the Security Council. Boldly, I argued that since our Ambassador to Zimbabwe had left his post following Zimbabwe's end of membership in the Security Council, we needed to maintain a high-level presence in the region, especially as South Africa was beginning to rejoin the international stage after the end of apartheid. Since the region at the time was not a sought-after one among colleagues, the idea of me relocating there appealed to the decision-makers. Shortly after my return to New York, I was informed of a pending ambassadorship, which would make me the first female ambassador from the State of Kuwait, or indeed from any of the countries that comprised the entire Gulf Cooperation Council.

At the time, I was in New York representing Kuwait in the eleven-member Sanctions Committee to monitor the supply and shipping of oil and petroleum products to South Africa. This was part of an overall attempt by the General Assembly to boycott South Africa in sports and investments. Then, prior to officially leaving New York for the start of my ambassadorship in Zimbabwe, I was instructed to join a Kuwaiti delegation led by Ali Al-Baghli, Minister of Oil, at the Minerals Engineering Conference in South Africa, in August 1993.

I arrived at Cape Town and prepared to receive the first-ever delegation from Kuwait to South Africa. It was a thrilling time, especially because many of the first-time attendees, including Kuwait, were members of the Non-Aligned Movement, who were staunch supporters of the boycott against apartheid South Africa. South African President de Klerk opened the conference, and our visit included a meeting of our delegation with African National Congress (ANC) leader Nelson Mandela at his hotel room. In one of my more vivid recollections, I remember Mandela greeting us in rather casual attire, shoeless because he was suffering from swollen feet. At one stage, he put on a beguiling smile and asked if we wanted a "family" photograph. I suddenly became the most popular member of the otherwise all-male delegation, being the only one with a camera.

"Family" photograph with delegation from Kuwait to South Africa. Nelson Mandela (seated, left), Ali Al-Baghli, Minister of Oil, (seated, right), Cape Town, South Africa (1993)

Among the leadership of the ANC, we also met Trevor Manuel, who at the time was responsible for economic affairs. The delegation did not mince words when pointing to the enormity of the task ahead as South Africa strived to meet national expectations for its post-apartheid participation on the international stage. Years later, Manuel would be appointed as Minister of Finance. I learned of this development while on a trip to Namibia, when a colleague told me that South Africa would finally have its first Black finance minister. I corrected him, pointing out that Trevor Manuel's complexion was fairer than mine and that being a member of the ANC did not mean that your skin color was necessarily black. We also met with the legendary Foreign Minister Pick Botha. I had been part of the Intergovernmental Group to Monitor the Supply of Oil and Petroleum products to South Africa, and Botha sounded ironic, but not unfriendly, when he remarked that after holding responsibility for monitoring the oil embargo against apartheid South Africa, we would now be engaged in the oil trade with the new South Africa. Of all of the meetings and interactions I recall, however, what stands out most in my mind today is the sense of harmony brought about by inviting Nelson Mandela to deliver the closing statement of the conference.

My relocation from New York to Harare took place four months later, in early January 1994, after a quick stopover in Kuwait for a swearing-in ceremony as Ambassador.

News of my designation was warmly welcomed and received in Kuwait and the wider region. Chief among those welcoming the news were members of Kuwait's Civil, Cultural, and Social Society, who held a reception in my honor and invited prominent men and women from the community. In retrospect, I was on such a fast track after designation as Ambassador-elect to a tremendously prestigious position that apart from events like this, I was left with little time to savor the full meaning of my change in status. However, I came to appreciate the fact that I was bestowed this responsibility due to my personal accomplishments rather than entitlement, and I will always be grateful to my leadership for conferring this honor upon me. No matter what status I had, I would always defer to my elders in the family, a humbling experience throughout my life. And so, upon leaving that special reception, I was quickly ushered into a waiting car by my older brother.

Swearing-in ceremony. Left to right: Sheikh Nasser Al-Mohammad Al-Sabah, Minister of the Amiri Diwan; Sheikh Sabah Al-Ahmad Al-Sabah, Minister of Foreign Affairs; me; His Highness the Amir Sheikh Jaber Al-Ahmad Al-Sabah, Kuwait City (1993)

Reception in my honor by the Kuwait Civil, Cultural, and Social Society, Kuwait City (1995)

Reception in my honor by the Kuwait Civil, Cultural, and Social Society, Kuwait City (1995)

Each country's protocol varies with respect to the presentation of credentials for an ambassador to a host country. I recall being quite anxious during my first experience in Zimbabwe, clutching my documents tightly as if my life depended on them. I was accompanied by a colleague from the embassy whose casual choice of attire further distressed me. I thought I should keep that in mind for the future to make sure our delegation would always represent our country in a formal and professional manner. The ceremony itself went smoothly until the President at the time, Robert Mugabe, noted that I was not helping myself to the tea during the private audience. I informed him that I was fasting, and he apologized for his insensitive staff who failed to let him know that it was Ramadan.

Now in Zimbabwe, I had to become acclimated to a different quality of life, having lived in New York for such a long period of time. The material luxury of the first world was supplanted by the luscious nature of the global south, which I had encountered during my first trip to Sub-Saharan Africa in 1985. I had visited Tanzania to see my friend, Salim Ahmed Salim, and his family, whom I had come to know closely during his tenure as Ambassador to the United Nations. He was the Tanzanian Minister of Interior at the time of my visit, and he welcomed me most graciously. The trip had left me with a positive impression of the region that would continue to build over the years, serving me well eight years later as I settled into life in Harare.

Kuwait greatly valued its relationship with Zimbabwe, and our relations were based on state-to-state collaboration, where Kuwait was a major donor to infrastructural projects, including the airport, small dams, and railways. It was part of the purview of the Kuwait Fund for Arab Economic Development (KFAED), a major state institution established in 1961 shortly after independence, to extend loans to developing countries, starting with loans to other Arab countries and slowly expanding to a more global reach. We were also a major supplier of oil and petroleum products to Zimbabwe, apart from an interruption in 1990 during the Iraqi invasion, when the UN sanctioned non-humanitarian imports to or from Iraq and occupied Kuwait. During that time, I was in New York and heavily involved in an appeal to the UN through the Sanctions Committee for the release of oil shipments already on the way to Zimbabwe and four other countries prior to the outbreak of hostilities on 2 August 1990. The shipment was seized by Yemen, an ally of Iraq at the time, while en route to its destinations. I actually appeared before the Sanctions Committee to call for release of the shipment, which had already been paid for.

For its part, Zimbabwe was a member of the Security Council from 1991–1992 and was quite supportive of our cause following the occupation by Iraq in 1990. They voted in favor of most of the resolutions presented in the Security Council, except the one that called for a no-fly zone in the north of Iraq to protect the Kurds from aerial attacks by Saddam's regime. Likewise, during our stint on the Security Council between 1978–1979, Kuwait had been supportive of Zimbabwe during the process to grant independence of what was then called Southern Rhodesia from the United Kingdom. At the time, I was a junior diplomat representing Kuwait in the

Non-Aligned Group, discussing the issue as the Kuwait government clarified its official stance. I remained non-committal and relegated myself to espousing Kuwait's general principles as we awaited further instruction. Unbeknownst to me, my statements were brought to the attention of the British Ambassador, who shocked me when he blurted out that I would be "held responsible for holding action by the Security Council to grant Zimbabwe membership at the UN." In reality it was not the Security Council's actions, or inaction, that delayed Zimbabwe's membership, but independence negotiations in Southern Rhodesia. I took umbrage at his remarks and sought reassurance from my Ambassador.

Of personal concern at the outset of my own first ambassadorship was the somewhat negative ambiance within the small Arab group of ambassadors. A number of them were fast on their feet to condemn military operations during the liberation of Kuwait in early 1991, seeking to influence the Zimbabwean government despite its historic support of Kuwait.

Zimbabwe was a very welcoming host country and provided me with a blessed reprieve from the hectic workload of the United Nations. My first week felt lonely, as I was on my own without family or personal staff. Compounding the feeling were the poor telephone lines, which meant I had no communication with the outside world. However, my stay was facilitated by the kind references my predecessor, Suheil, had shared with his colleagues. The advice from him and his wife guided me towards a quality of life that I came to enjoy in the country. Admittedly, I missed some luxuries, particularly sources of information that were readily available in New York.

Above all, I used to be frustrated when the satellite system or landline went off during the rainy season. Mobile telephones were still unavailable in Zimbabwe, leaving me quite starved for news during those periods. My solace came in the form of telexes from the Kuwait News Agency, which I willingly shared with colleagues in a similar predicament, riding my bicycle and delivering the scrolls to neighboring residences. Little did I know that it was not becoming of an Ambassador to cycle around like a paperboy, handing out news clippings.

I had begun the process of settling into my new position as Ambassador, which included making the customary courtesy calls to other colleagues. On one such visit to my American colleague, he presented me with a handwritten letter by his immediate boss, Ambassador April Glaspie. She had warm words about my historic appointment and even requested the Ambassador to present me with a bouquet of flowers. April had made headlines as the American Ambassador to Iraq leading up to the 1990 invasion and had since then maintained a low profile but was given a role in the State Department. Nevertheless, our roads did occasionally cross; she joined me and several Kuwaiti friends at a private dinner in DC in late 1990, participated at the UN as a member of the US delegation, in the US State Department responsible for Africa, and later served as Consul General of the US in South Africa.

Although it was initially challenging to arrive in Harare without family or staff, I eventually learned to manage. Running an entire embassy was a completely different experience from simply working in one. It filled me with appreciation and marvel for the amount of work my mother put into running our household. I was soon rewarded by visits from family and friends who made the long trip to keep me company and explore a country that would normally not have appeared on their radar as a travel destination. I took it upon myself to really explore the country and traveled to far-flung locations, not content to remain within the confines of Harare. While Victoria Falls was the iconic attraction for most of my guests, I also introduced them to a remote site called Vumba. This small rainforest near Mozambique's border is home to a quaint castle built, as the narrative goes, by Italian prisoners of war who were captured by the British during World War II. Also of interest to some visitors was the tobacco auction floor, where the process of bringing the tobacco to viewing and then to sale is concluded within twenty-four hours. I took family and friends to visit Bulawayo, the second-largest town in Zimbabwe. Everyone was interested in the cotton industry of the country. It was a marvel to know that some local companies were catering to the likes of Bloomingdale's and Banana Republic, and on the way to visit some of the cotton factories, we visited Cecil Rhodes' burial place, a marvel of a sight at the top of a hill!

Zimbabwe provided a gentle learning curve for a female Ambassador, which served me well, as I was experienced in some ways, yet still green in others. Early on, for example, a friendly Eastern European colleague advised me to be constantly accompanied by an assistant in order to keep up appearances befitting the status of Ambassador. Then once, as a Muslim woman accustomed to Kuwait's mosques, where women are allotted a space inside the mosque, I endeavored to visit the main mosque in Harare, only to be abruptly waved away and told that women were only hosted in a small adjacent building. This experience dampened my resolve to visit local mosques in future postings, preferring to relegate that duty to a male colleague. I was also left with a permanent dent on my psyche as I encountered the importance of a spouse in supporting an ambassador's life and career. On this note, I came to appreciate the women who had to relinquish a career back home to be with their diplomat husbands, and who were not allowed to work in a host country even on a voluntary basis.

As I spent more time in Zimbabwe, I became aware of the distinct roles of women and men in Zimbabwean society. Once, when I was walking through a local street market, I was captivated by a stone sculpture depicting a woman balancing a basket on her head. I wanted to commission him to sculpt a male partner for this piece, but the shocked vendor to whom I made this request informed me that men do not carry loads on their heads. He eventually relented, and I then placed the pair of sculptures in the dining area of the residence supporting a glass tabletop, where they were often a conversation piece.

Hand-sculpted stone figures,
Zimbabwe (2005)

Outside of anything to do with gender roles, I also came to appreciate the impact that personal initiatives could have in unexpected circumstances. Like those in other countries in the region, HIV-infected youth in Zimbabwe were stigmatized and found it difficult to thrive in such a negative environment. Through a personal initiative, I contacted private Kuwaiti citizens who were willing to help and facilitated the donation of funds to help support these youths. Another disadvantaged group were those who had lost limbs to landmines in the struggle for freedom. This was a cause that I could get behind, as supplying them with artificial limbs was not a great expense. Upon my request, a good friend and relation promptly advanced money in support of this project.

Of course, most of my efforts were focused on more official duties. Shortly after arrival to the country, I attended to arrangements for celebrating Kuwait's National Day, my first as a Head of Mission. I dove into the preparations, eager to hit the ground running. It is the norm at these events to play the national anthems of both countries. Unimpressed with the themes that the army band played, I requested that they also play some music by Glenn Miller. Big bands and live music have a certain charm with a crowd, and the evening was a success!

Botswana

While in Harare, I was also designated as Non-resident Ambassador to Botswana, marking the first time that Botswana hosted an Ambassador for Kuwait. My accreditation to Botswana was a surreal one, since on my way to the airport I was asked by the Ambassador of Botswana to delay the presentation until we announced the establishment of relations. Nevertheless, I was thrilled to receive this historic post, knowing that, just as with Zimbabwe, our two countries enjoyed close collaboration through KFAED. President Festus Mogae, who was gracious enough to recognize Kuwait's assistance before we even had diplomatic relations, granted me an audience. Like Zimbabwe, Botswana was supportive of Kuwait during the occupation by Iraq. They even requested an interview with a Kuwaiti diplomat for their national radio during the occupation. In fact, President Mogae of Botswana spoke at length on Kuwait's historical support of the country during the presentation of my credentials, our countries' relationship taking on a "human face" as he shared the details of this bond during our meeting.

Apparently Kuwait had introduced Botswana to the mechanism of the OPEC Fund and other donor institutions, including the World Bank. The President himself visited Kuwait in the 1980s when he was a member of the cabinet. Kuwait's institutions would prove to be just as effective, if not more so, as its diplomatic representations. I say that in recognition of the remarkable work by KFAED within the South African Development Community (SADC) and the greater region. SADC routinely includes KFAED in the annual meetings that I used to trudge along to. I learned a lot from them and enjoyed being introduced to the mechanism of their work in host countries. Much depended on cordial relations between outgoing and incoming ambassadors, as well as among officials, and I noted a lack of networking between institutions and an inability to centralize and make available information and data concerning other states.

One of the most memorable incidents was a visit to western Botswana to assess the viability of a road project adjacent to the San tribal land, close to Namibia. It was a visit by a technical team that I was glad to be included in, as the area was remote and out of the general sphere or scope of locations I would visit for work. After powering through dirt roads and dealing with a couple of flat tires, we were rewarded by the warm welcome of the San tribal leaders.

Presenting my credentials to President Festus Mogae, Botswana (1995)

Another time, I officially participated in the opening ceremony of a highway connecting the capital of Gaborone to the
border with Namibia. It was not only the Fund, but also two
Kuwaiti companies who were active in the project, in addition
to financing from Japan and the EU. I have often wondered
at the close coordination that donor institutions enjoy in the
field, while they fail to collaborate at the initial drawing board.
It is as though field work takes precedence over the behind-
the-scenes coordination that necessarily precedes it. I followed
this issue in earnest later when in Brussels, as the EU always
seemed keen to include Kuwait and other Gulf donors in their
assistance programs, while at the same time imposing restric-
tive and costly guidelines. This relationship between KFAED
and Botswana continued to grow in subsequent years as road
and railway links were deemed vital for infrastructural development in the country.

South Africa

My first year in Zimbabwe coincided with the inauguration of Nelson Mandela as President of South Africa in 1994.
Kuwait did not yet have diplomatic relations with the new
Black-majority government in South Africa, as the country
had just undergone elections. I was to attend the inauguration
and receive the official delegation from Kuwait. I was quite
nervous about the task, as I had no base or staff to help facilitate this visit and instead had to rely on assistance from the
South African authorities.

The inauguration at the Union Building in Pretoria was

the largest-ever gathering of international leaders on South African soil. The banquet that followed was the envy of any event planner for its grandeur and class, only to be outdone years later during the celebration of Mandela's 80th birthday and his wedding ceremony to Graça Machel, his longtime partner. On the way to the inauguration, Sheikh Sabah inquired if we had found a residence for the Kuwait embassy. He was surprised to learn that the groundwork of recognition between the two countries and my nomination as Ambassador were not on track. As usual, with directives from the top, it suddenly became a priority, and I found myself adding South Africa to my list of non-residency ambassadorial posts. The presentation of my credentials took place shortly thereafter, together with eighteen colleagues from other nations who also assumed their posts.

At the time, it was the largest contingent of would-be ambassadors ever received by a Head of State. During the private audience, which is usually a ceremonial one, I was surprised that President Mandela chose to inject a reference to a telephone conversation with President Bush on the military operations to liberate Kuwait. He added that he was not in agreement with the use of force against a non-aligned country, upon which I retorted that the people of South Africa had to resort to force in order to make dents in the apartheid regime, while Kuwait relied on the United Nations to do so. I believe that encounter made an impression, and I enjoyed his warm remarks about me in the days to follow.

Months later, in Harare, I received a call, presumably from Mandela's office, and heard his voice inviting me to lunch. I was wary because it was around the same time that a radio host had impersonated the Canadian prime minister to solicit support from Queen Elizabeth. In case the call I received was a scam, I responded that I would need some time to travel from Harare to Pretoria for the lunch. I eventually found out that the invitation was valid, and I did go and had a memorable time. President Mandela shared his plans for a trip to Kuwait and inquired into why Harare was my base. I told him that if Kuwait had a residence in Pretoria like the Union Building, I would be back immediately with carry-on luggage.

Inauguration of President Nelson Mandela, Pretoria, South Africa. Front row, left to right: Khaled Al-Jarallah, Undersecretary of the Foreign Ministry; Ambassador Abdullah Bishara; Ambassador Sheikh Sabah Al-Ahmad Al-Sabah, Deputy Prime Minister and Minister of Foreign Affairs; and me (1994)

Nabeela Al Mulla

*Presenting my credentials to President Nelson Mandela,
Pretoria, South Africa (1994)*

Private lunch with President Mandela, Pretoria (1994)

Staying the Course in Southern Africa with a Move to Pretoria

During my time as Ambassador to Zimbabwe and Non-resident Ambassador to Botswana and South Africa, I was tapped as a potential Ambassador to Turkey. I felt uneasy about the rationale for the relocation, given that no successor for my posts in Southern Africa was envisioned in the near future. It may have just been a passing notion on the part of the Kuwaiti government, however, for nothing came of the idea. I stayed the course in Southern Africa and added two countries to my portfolio, Namibia and Mauritius.

While I felt committed to my diplomatic posts in Southern Africa, I was still listed as Deputy Permanent Representative to the Mission in New York. During a visit to the UN in early 1995, I was alerted by an American colleague in Washington that my dual representation was raising eyebrows. Armed with this warning, my name was eventually taken off the list of diplomatic staff at the Mission.

Zimbabwe was certainly a marvel of a country, but it failed in its capacity to emerge as a viable regional leader. Up-and-coming South Africa instead settled into that role, stirring up an underlying competition that would define the relationship between these two countries, evidence of which I saw up close on a few occasions. For example, I witnessed an exchange during the first meeting of the SADC attended by Presidents Nelson Mandela and Robert Mugabe. My colleagues and I were astonished when Mugabe announced at the public meeting the idea for an African peacekeeping force. In this line

of work, ideas and policies, no matter how beneficial or positive they may be, must be introduced in a manner that will
garner understanding and support. Mandela politely brushed
the issue aside. The timing was not right, and especially in the
world of diplomacy, timing is of the essence.

Given South Africa's emergence as regional leader, it was
clear by 1996 that I should relocate to Pretoria. Back then,
South Africa was coping with an influx of diplomats, primarily
from non-aligned countries, and others who boycotted apartheid South Africa. My move was far from smooth, as there was
no support staff to assist me. On the eve of my arrival, I independently started the formal process of notifying the other
embassies that Kuwait had established a resident embassy
in Pretoria. At the time, my tools included a personal type-
writer, fax machine, a list of foreign embassies, and some official stationery pre-ordered from headquarters. Thankfully, this
bare-boned welcome to a new posting would not be repeated
later in my career.

Newcomers to the country lacked the luxury that their
predecessors had in terms of an additional Cape Town residence and staff, a remnant of the lifestyle of the then predominantly white officialdom. Eventually Pretoria would gain
weight as the center of political power, and that is where I was
satisfied to establish an office and residence, both of historical significance, in a relatively short time. I relish the sense of
history, wherever that may be, and this was no different. The
office building was purchased from a white South African who
decided to relocate to a predominantly white area. The archi-
tect was the renowned Herbert Baker, of Anglo-Saxon descent,

who had also designed the Union Building, the Ypres Memorial in Belgium, and the Parliament in New Delhi. The residence itself used to be the seat of the bishop of the Anglican Church and to this day bears a plaque reading that the royal family received the Most Holy Sacrament there on Easter Day, 1947.

IN THIS CHAPEL,
ON EASTER DAY 1947,
THEIR MAJESTIES,
KING GEORGE AND QUEEN ELIZABETH
WITH THE PRINCESSES
ELIZABETH AND MARGARET,
RECEIVED
THE MOST HOLY SACRAMENT.

Plaque at Kuwait Ambassador Residence in Pretoria, South Africa

Moving to the new residence from a temporary rental in Pretoria was taxing. It was the end of the year, close to the holiday season, and I had plans to leave with my niece Rula to London. Ever the organizer, she advised that we finish the move. "We set the deadline; we can change it" were her wise words.

During my early days of getting settled, KFAED was planning to attend a SADC conference to take place in Pretoria. I
picked up the representative from the airport in my 4-wheel
drive vehicle. He thought this was a cool thing for an Ambassador to do, until he realized I had only done so because I
had no driver. Nevertheless, we discussed the importance of
making inroads into South Africa's infrastructural development. That proved to be a tough case to follow, as the country's new leadership seemed to lack an understanding of the
need to diversify sources for economic development. At times,
it appeared as if the issue at hand was national pride rather
than exigency. Our private sector, however, was able to quickly
establish a modest presence in the country, which cemented
our burgeoning relationship.

My South African staff, if one could call it that, was a skeleton crew I managed with the addition of an able deputy.
The diplomatic corps was noticeably larger than the one in
Zimbabwe and included a sizable Arab group with whom I
was able to collaborate. The Egyptian Ambassador Mushira, in
particular, was of great assistance in facilitating my welcome to
Pretoria. I was also fortunate to reconnect with former Emirati
and British colleagues who had served at the United Nations at
the same time I did. The most striking reunion was the newly
appointed American Consul General in Cape Town, April
Glaspie. She was in her element in the Cape. Female ambassadors were a scant four, but the spouses made quite an interesting lot.

With Andrew Young at my residence in Pretoria, South Africa (1997)

During my stay in the city, I partook in two memorable weddings. One was that of the iconic American Ambassador Andrew Young to his second wife in 1996. The ceremony was held in Cape Town at the residence of the American Ambassador to South Africa and officiated by the Reverend Bishop Tutu. It was a fairly small wedding that Young endeavored to hold in lieu of a grander one in his hometown of Atlanta, Georgia. I held a dinner in his honor in my modest residence and hired a jazz band to perform. My good friend's son, Madani Adjali, was visiting at the time and proved to be a great co-host.

Another memorable wedding I attended was that of President Nelson Mandela to his partner Graça Machel, widow of the former President of Mozambique, which coincided with Mandela's 80th birthday in 1998. Together with the rest of the diplomatic corps, I was one of some 2,000 guests in the sprawling, makeshift grounds near Johannesburg. Nina Simone, Michael Jackson, and Stevie Wonder entertained the vibrant crowd in attendance. Also attending the event was Prince Bandar bin Sultan, who had worked closely with Mandela to resolve the Lockerbie plane crash that Libya was accused of masterminding.

Needless to say, South Africa was an interesting place in every sense of the word, possessing a beautiful landscape that stretched from the Indian Ocean to the Atlantic. Practically a new nation, it was charting its way internally and with the outside world, endowed with natural resources and with a sizeable bureaucracy striving to steer the country forward after decades of isolation in the international fora. I recall the head of my delegation, Ali Al-Baghli, Minister for Oil, telling the ANC official for Economic Affairs before independence, Trevor Manuel, that his position would dramatically change from that of spectator to player in the field. He warned Manuel that people would expect immediate gratification upon the ANC assuming power, and that the challenges would be immense. Manuel eventually assumed the post of Minister of Finance and was one of the first officials I met after I moved to Pretoria. When I explained to him Kuwait's policy of collaborating with developing countries in infrastructure projects, he did not seem receptive. One South African official privately murmured that some of his own senior officials would need to learn some humility in the process. Upon relaying this message back to Kuwait, I was advised to bide my time.

Another person who had a profound impact on South African politics before and after apartheid was Bishop Tutu.

His stewardship of the Truth and Reconciliation Commission was a landmark in the politics of the country after apartheid. The process was free of external guidelines and provided people from all ethnic groups with opportunities to share their experiences under apartheid. As a member of the diplomatic corps, I attended the opening of the commission's work and followed its proceedings. It made such an impression on me that I later referred EU officials to it as an example to be emulated in Iraq after the 2003 war.

In 1997 I was fortunate to attend the 50th ANC Conference in Mafikeng, where ANC leadership would elect their next leader, Thabo Mbeki, to succeed Mandela. It was an internal affair with few outsiders in attendance. The venue was not equipped to handle the influx of foreign delegates, but I managed to acquire modest lodgings with the help of some friends in the ANC. I recall the buzz that surrounded the arrival of Nelson Mandela's estranged wife, Winnie Mandela, to the conference.

Around this time, one Kuwaiti official advised me to meet the King of the Zulu nation. A 48-hour adventure to a remote part of South Africa transpired. An old ANC friend from New York organized the meeting and accompanied me. I met the King the next day and presented him with a small gift, a model of a Kuwaiti dhow, a sailing vessel. Whether or not the landlocked King of the Zulu appreciated the gift of a ship, I cannot be certain; however, I found him quite charming and well spoken.

In 1998 I attended the 12th Non-Aligned Movement (NAM) Summit in Durban, with Sheikh Sabah leading the delegation. I encountered a number of logistical challenges around hotel rooms and workstations, which underscored the complexities of attending to a delegation, particularly in an unfamiliar setting. Amusingly, I had to argue with the hotel staff to let my cook use their facilities, where his cooking skills earned him the respect of the hotel staff and a special apron acknowledging his role as the "NAM Summit Chef." In June 1999 Sheikh Sabah attended the inauguration of South African President Thabo Mbeki, echoing his attendance at Mandela's inauguration in 1995.

Presenting the King of the Zulu with a Kuwaiti dhow, South Africa (1997)

*Photo of the underplate during President Nelson Mandela's
80th birthday and wedding, Pretoria, South Africa (1998)*

Namibia

Settling in Pretoria allowed me to cover Namibia, another African country whose aspiration for independence was a focus of international attention when I was at the UN. Namibia had a special place in my career, dating back to the years of 1978–1979 when the Security Council was working in earnest to resolve the country's occupation by apartheid South Africa. On a personal level, I had befriended Theo-Ben Gurirab, the representative of the SWAPO freedom movement to the UN, who later became the first Namibian Minister of Foreign Affairs following independence from South Africa.

I had first presented my credentials to Namibian President Sam Nujoma in 1994, at a time when Iraq was amassing troops near Kuwait's border despite international sanctions. The ceremony was a collective one, involving a number of other ambassadors; however, I was later summoned to a private audience where President Nujoma expressed concern at the turn of events and solidarity with Kuwait. He had a congenial character, and I commented that I might be visiting places in his country he had not seen yet, as he had been in exile until independence in March 1990.

Then, in 1996, I traveled to Walvis Bay, whose sovereignty was contested with South Africa, and I cut short my intended itinerary when told that President Nujoma requested my company for lunch in nearby Windhoek. This was an honor I could not refuse! As we talked over our meal, I slowly came to understand that he held my Head of State, Sheikh Jaber Al-Ahmad Al-Sabah, in high esteem for His Highness' discrete assistance to SWAPO's struggle for independence from apartheid South Africa. This was not public knowledge, nor was I briefed about it before going to Windhoek. I also mentioned my interest in visiting the Fish River Canyon on my way back to my residency in South Africa.

During the lunch, the topic of the Kuwaiti oil delegation, which was supposed to visit Namibia in July 1990, was brought up. Namibia was interested in engaging Kuwait to develop oil deposits in the country. It came to naught, as Kuwaiti officials were deeply involved in fending off Iraqi claims prior to its invasion of Kuwait on 2 August 1990.

Meeting with President Sam Njouma of Namibia (1994)

I thoroughly enjoyed my time in Namibia, despite how brief it was. I was invited to a showcase of a unique marble factory, where I marveled at the rich lapis lazuli and other precious stones. These raw products were often shipped to Europe to be transformed into luxury products. I managed to find a small outlet that manufactured them at a reasonable cost. I also appreciated being part of the KFAED team that surveyed by air the enigmatic Skeleton Coast to pre-assess the viability of developing a port in the northwestern part of the country. Being in Namibia reminded me of a time at the UN when I had the privilege of delivering Kuwait's speech welcoming the release of the Namibian freedom fighter Toivo ya Toivo from sixteen years' incarceration in Robben Island. He became Minister of Minerals upon independence.

Speech at the United Nations General Assembly welcoming the release of Toivo ya Toivo, New York (1984)

During a farewell visit to Namibia in 1999, recognizing their initial reluctance to cosponsor a British-Dutch draft at the UN Security Council on Iraq, I argued for broader support to lend credibility, and they eventually accepted my rationale.

Mauritius

The last posting with which I was entrusted was to the beautiful island nation of Mauritius, in the Indian Ocean, over 3,500 kilometers from South Africa. It had the advantage of enjoying a harmonious social mix and vibrant economy, especially during the apartheid period, when South African businesses established roots there in order to avoid sanctions. Our relationship with Mauritius was smooth, and they availed themselves of economic assistance by KFAED in some projects. My presence on the island was limited to official occasions in order to enhance the political aspect of the relationship. I timed visits from the family to coincide with my working trips to the island so that they could partake and share in its beauty. The only instance of political drama during the posting came about when I had to defend Kuwait's actions in the Sanctions Committee on Iraq regarding the oil supply that was due to arrive in Zimbabwe and Mauritius, among other countries, and which was seized by Yemen.

While I was accredited to Mauritius, I learned that a Parliamentary delegation was planning to visit the island. Despite feeling compelled to accompany them out of a sense of duty, I was unable to do so, due to a previously scheduled engagement with officials in Cape Town. In my stead, I delegated the visit to my deputy, the only other diplomat from Kuwait in the region.

Out of Africa

Towards the end of my sixth year in Southern Africa, I was contacted by a colleague at another post who advised me that being out of sight or off the radar of high officials might be a rationale to prolong my assignment in the region. Another colleague commented that being in the Southern Hemisphere gives the impression that one is far removed from the politics taking part on the main stage. One colleague admonished me, asking if I watched the news as the Japanese embassy in Peru was stormed and the Ambassador taken. I was definitely out of the loop! These were timely wake-up calls as I weighed my options for a future that would be equally challenging and interesting. I needed to softly nudge and inform the Foreign Ministry that I was not averse to being relocated to another post.

With some hesitation, I took action and contacted a decision-maker within the Ministry to say that I would be open to a new post closer to home. Soon after, I was informed that my next posting would be in Vienna as Ambassador to Austria and various multilateral organizations, where my previous experience in New York would play to my advantage in the historic Habsburg capital. Indeed, leaving the African continent meant also leaving behind the only truly bilateral postings of my career. The only taste of multilateralism during this period was my cursory engagement with the KFAED in attending ceremonial meetings with the SADC, where they led Kuwait's representation and I took a backseat.

I readied myself and did my rounds of official farewells in

Southern Africa, only to have the move put on freeze. Apparently, in the chain of shifting ambassadors, there was one person who had issues relating to his children's schooling. Being single presumably meant to some that I had no family obligations, and I had to wait until early December 1999.

Throughout my tour of duty in the Southern African region, I never encountered raised eyebrows over my position as a woman ambassador from my region. I was accepted as I was and welcomed as an ambassador of a country enjoying friendly relations with the host countries, not as a phenomenon or a celebrity. This attitude has perhaps had a positive impact on my psyche and helped me to carry myself with humility. My circumstances and reception would differ greatly during my later tours of duty in the developed world, where I often seemed to be viewed as an anomaly to the standards they thought our region held. Such an attitude prompted me to be critical of the standard bearers, the West, or any of the countries in the developed world that measured other countries based on their own preconceived notions and stereotypes.

I did not immediately anticipate these difficulties once my assignment to Vienna was official, but I did regard my planned departure from Southern Africa as a welcome change. My term of duty in the region, especially my post in South Africa, was an enriching and unforgettable experience. Together with Namibia, South Africa was among the last major countries to shed the shackles of a long colonial hegemony as the majority of the countries of the African continent had gained their independence in the 1960s and 1970s. Like the rest of my generation in the developing world, I identified with their struggle for freedom and democracy. I was attracted to, and keen to meet, a number of those public figures who made those dreams reality and whom I'd only heard of in history books. Among these exceptional individuals was the late Walter Sisulu, a close friend and mentor of Nelson Mandela. With the help of an ANC female colleague, I was thrilled to visit Walter Sisulu and his wife, Albertina, in 1997 in their modest home in the township of Soweto, where he returned to live after over twenty years of incarceration in Robben Island prison. He was quite frail and, despite the acclaim that followed him, modest. One would find it difficult not to be humbled in his presence, and I would count this visit among the most cherished memories of my post in South Africa.

Visit to the home of Walter Sisulu in Soweto, South Africa. Left to right: ANC friend, Albertina Sisulu, Walter Sisulu, me (1997)

I would also treasure the times I shared with family and friends in the region when they visited me. I was not the only one captivated with the natural beauty of the region. Embarking on safari excursions with my family and friends created enduring memories for my visitors and for me as host. Whether traversing the untamed landscapes of Zimbabwe with my close friend Sonia and her husband, Eddie, exploring the wilderness of South Africa with my family, or venturing into the heart of Botswana alongside Madani, Boubaker Adjali's son, each safari was a unique adventure. Steering clear of the over-commercialized routes, I opted for more authentic experiences, relying on local connections to recommend hidden gems for accommodations. From the rugged safaris along the Zambezi River with Madani, to the mesmerizing journey to the Indian Ocean with my niece Rula, which included turtle watching. I also took breathtaking boat safaris in Lake Kariba with my older sister, Moudhi, my close friend Mary, and her little girl, Alyssa. My late brother Lutfi and his wife Shrouk joined me on one of my expeditions flying over a diverse array of terrains. Navigating air, land, and waterways with small planes, riverboats, cars, and 4x4s, each mode of transport added an element of excitement to our explorations. In preparation for these thrilling excursions, I often sought guidance from locals, ensuring a deeper connection with the land and its people. The result was an exhilarating period of discovery and bonding with loved ones amid the captivating landscapes of Africa.

Relocating from South Africa was memorable to say the least. By the end of my term in the region, I had amassed quite an inventory of memorabilia, especially artwork, which would overwhelm any single logistical planner. Family volunteered their time and energy to assist in the packing. While I had initially traveled to the region on my own with no staff to speak of, I departed with three household staff members who would stay with me throughout my future postings. That consistency and support confirmed for me that relocating from one post to another need not be traumatic if one is tuned to adapting to the novelty. The common adage is that one needs six months to take in the new surroundings, adapt to the pace of work, and establish contacts.

Once in Vienna, I found myself surrounded by friends and family celebrating the turn of the millennium in the hometown of an Austrian friend. How stark a difference the transition would be when compared to my beginnings in Southern Africa.

Moving North

The history of military conflict in Afghanistan [has] been one of initial success, followed by long years of floundering and ultimate failure. We're not going to repeat that mistake.
—President George W. Bush
April 17, 2002

I was thrilled to learn that The Three Tenors were performing the same week of my arrival in Vienna. I had attended a remarkable performance by the trio at Union Building in Pretoria, and seeing them perform again in Austria provided me with a warm thread of consistency during a time of upheaval.

At any new station, it is necessary to use all tools available to ensure that you know the correct and most effective method for approaching your new hosts. There is no universal handbook. Throughout one's career, attention to details of decorum sometimes escapes one. Indeed, this happened later in my career twice when I failed to read the small print about the presentation of credentials in the Bahamas, and again in Belgium. I often wondered at the mishaps that I could fall into if I failed to follow such guidance.

As in Botswana, I was not formally alerted in advance to such details when I received my posting in Austria. Luckily, an Austrian colleague whom I met in Zimbabwe advised me on the best course of action in his country, noting that in addition to credentials, I was expected to deliver my own personal message to the President. It was time to go into overdrive. I reached out to friends to come up with ideas that would be interesting to share during my first encounter with then President Thomas Klestil. In the process, I learned that Kuwaiti companies were importing tree pulp from Austria instead of from the more common suppliers in the Nordic countries. I also learned that the use of silver coins called the Maria-Theresa thaler was widespread in financial transactions in old Kuwait. Background knowledge like this helped facilitate a smooth and enjoyable meeting. I also learned that President Klestil had been Ambassador to the United Nations, and he was impressed by the length of my tenure there compared to his. Over the years, I came to appreciate the fact that the UN posting is a common denominator for many career diplomats and officials.

At one time, being the only woman ambassador in the Arab group was not so welcoming. There was an instance when the governor of one of the rural provinces invited the group for a long weekend. I hastily stated that the invitation must naturally include spouses, a sentiment not appreciated by some of my colleagues. I was fortunate, however, to have a number of competent colleagues able to assist me in getting settled in Austria. Jokingly, I liked to refer to them as my "three kings." I was also blessed to have a female colleague join me at this posting. Reem Al-Khaled proved to be the three kings' professional equal.

Presentation of my credentials to President Thomas Klestil in the presence of my "three kings," Vienna, Austria (2000)

The Kuwait Residence in Austria was a "petite palais" that had been occupied by the SS during World War II. During my stay there, I unearthed a deep, wide tunnel that spanned the grounds to the neighboring streets. It must have been quite a sight for my team, watching me descend a rickety ladder to explore a strange tunnel underneath the house. Certainly not elegant for an Ambassador! Above ground, adapting to the Austrian winter from the South African summer was cumbersome to say the least, but I soon became oblivious to the weather when confronted with the colossal number of tasks to be performed. First and foremost, I had to establish my presence in Austria and lay a foundation before branching off to the various international organizations and neighboring countries. There would also be occasions for less formal engagements that were nevertheless valuable. In 2001, for example, a Kuwaiti private individual sought assistance for media coverage of a skiing event in St. Anton, representing Kuwait among sixty nations. I remember thinking how important it was to have representation in such international events.

My arrival in Austria coincided with the ascendancy of the right-wing populist Freedom Party, led by Dr. Jörg Haider, who seemed to use any occasion to try and flex his muscles—even ones where I believed he was unwelcome. The Chancellor took his time to form a coalition government, at first refusing to accept the inclusion of the Freedom Party. Finally, he had to relent, causing quite a stir within the European Union. As a direct result of a far-right party within the government of Austria, the EU embarked on the unprecedented response of freezing diplomatic relations with the country. This was a rare procedure that seemed to disrupt the political fabric among Europeans. I learned of this freeze firsthand—sort of. At the time, Portugal held the presidency of the EU, and I had called their Ambassador in Vienna for a completely unrelated subject. He informed me that he was instructed to cancel an upcoming major cultural event by Portugal in Vienna. I was surprised by this news because he had earlier shared his excitement about the exhibition, which centered on Portuguese explorations and their historic colonial outreach in the world. Ultimately, the event took place, but it was much subdued and without any fanfare. Austria was simply not to be celebrated or feted as an EU member. That sanction decision, which took place over a weekend in February 2000, was later scrutinized and criticized for the hasty manner in which it was implemented. It was quite an experience, one that foreshadowed the rise of populist governments over the following decades.

Dr. Haidar, however, did not miss a beat and relished any opportunity to ingratiate himself in the diplomatic world. Carinthia being his hometown, he made sure that he and the press were front and center to meet and greet OPEC finance ministers at a regular meeting, planned in advance in different provinces of Austria. I had other brushes with the Freedom Party, including an invitation to attend Saif Al-Islam Gaddafi's matriculation celebration, which I evaded by begging a commitment in neighboring Slovakia. In another instance, I was invited to join Dr. Haidar at the Vienna Opera Ball, the mother of all balls, where Saif Al-Islam was purported to be in attendance along with a number of other dignitaries. Once more, I claimed commitments in one of the other countries for which I was responsible and managed to deftly avoid what would undoubtedly have been an awkward evening.

The final straw was Dr. Haidar's attempt to endear himself to Iraq and Kuwait by offering to mediate on the issue of our prisoners of war held by Iraq. I assured him, in my most diplomatic way, that there was already an international mechanism dealing with the issue and that Kuwait trusted that mechanism. He did not offer his services again.

During my term of duty in Austria, I had opportunities to witness the inner workings of OPEC and the OPEC Fund, which are normally in the domain of oil and finance ministers, respectively. KFAED was quite active in these fora, and given my close relationship with the Fund from my time in Southern Africa, I was included in the delegation during their deliberations. It was an enriching experience to witness at close range the decision-making process of a major financial institution that impacted our policy in developing countries. It allowed member countries to extend financial assistance to infrastructural projects in countries without the national constraints normally associated with one's foreign policy.

Decision-making at OPEC was a different ballgame altogether. Calling the shots were usually major producers, primarily Saudi Arabia, in consultation with others. I was privy to that process, due to my close relationship with Sheikh Soud Nasser Al-Sabah, Minister of Oil, who was previously a career diplomat.

This close relationship followed with the subsequent Kuwaiti oil ministers. Once due to the inadvertent absence of our oil minister, the responsibility of leading the delegation was entrusted to me. It was an overwhelming and daunting task, since other members of the delegation were better versed on agenda matters. Naturally, I deferred to their advice and kept a demeanor of confidence leading the delegation. It was also a photo opportunity for a delegation led by three women: the Ambassador; Governor Siham Razzouki; and the National Representative to OPEC, Nawal Al-Fezai.

With Sheikh Saud Nasser Al-Sabah, Minister of Oil, at the OPEC meeting in Vienna, Austria (2000)

*OPEC Delegation in Vienna. Left to right: Governor Siham
Razzouki, me, and Nawal Al-Fezai, National Representative
to OPEC (2002)*

Austria, being a bilateral and multilateral host country, had
quite a number of women heads of mission. My customary
courtesy calls included the Dean of Women Ambassadors,
Thelma Doran, who was overly welcoming and resourceful.
Being from Ireland, I benefited from her insights on the Western
group. Instead of a customary courtesy call to the office, she
invited me to lunch. I would borrow this practice several times
throughout my career. During my chairmanship of the Board of
Governors of the IAEA, only one other delegation, Argentina,
was headed by a woman. Kuwait's own delegation included the
very capable Reem Al-Khaled, who later spread her wings and

acquired an ambassadorial assignment. Included among the interesting women who were part of the various delegations were a Lebanese diplomat, Caroline Ziadeh, who was quite proficient in her grasp of issues; and the Israeli representative, who was a scientist rather than a career diplomat. The latter was tactful and refrained from direct contact with me in my capacity as Chairman. Despite that, I could not help but get nervous every time she went around the chamber contacting other delegates, because I did not know what she was planning. Of the array of women I encountered during my one year as Chairman, I was fascinated by the IAEA Egyptian inspector, who was among the lot who were expelled from the DPRK in late 2002. I met with her personally to express my admiration for an Arab woman who had an arduous task in what was considered a hardship post. To this day, I often cite her as an example of women's empowerment.

In addition to my appointment as Ambassador to Austria, I was nominated to represent Kuwait in Hungary, Slovenia, and Slovakia on a non-residency basis. I joked with friends that if the Czech Republic were thrown in, I would have an empire as my domain of duties. I was personally relieved that one scheduled audience to present credentials to the Hungarian President coincided with another event where I was requested to represent Kuwait, a conference of democracies hosted in Poland and chaired by Secretary of State Madeleine Albright. I personally did not think that these conferences added anything of note towards the grand purpose of shoring up democracy or the rule of law in the world, and so I was glad that the presentation of credentials took priority. Ambassadors do not usually air sentiments of this kind; we are expected to go along with the directives unless there is some overwhelming rationale against it.

My presentation of credentials to the three bordering states was always in the company of another colleague. It was done with flair and in an organized manner, a stark contrast to my African postings, where I was on my own to see the Head of State. In the case of South Africa, hotel employees saw me off to the event! During that time, none of the European countries where I held diplomatic posts were members of the EU, much less the Schengen Area, yet traveling was smooth and my tasks were facilitated by friendly relations between the host countries and Kuwait. Hungary, for example, was one of the countries that assisted in putting out the oil fires set by Saddam Hussein's regime upon the Iraqi retreat from Kuwait.

In Slovenia, Kuwait participated in the International Trust Fund for Demining project as a donor country, and I traveled there with Reem Al-Khaled to attend some sessions. As one of the former states that emerged relatively unscathed from the breakup of Yugoslavia, I enjoyed the natural beauty of the country. My responsibilities in Slovakia, on the other hand, were cumbersome due to an unprecedented influx of students with various problems, and issues with compatriots who were unfamiliar with the novelty of residency and accreditation. I also recall having to open the embassy on a holiday in order to issue visas so that Slovak military personnel could join the coalition of the willing during the American invasion of Iraq in 2003.

While I was very busy with official duties in Austria and in my posts in neighboring countries, being in Vienna afforded me the added luxury of proximity to the arts in the form of museums, balls, and cultural events.

Opening an art exhibition at OPEC Fund headquarters in Vienna, Austria (2003)

*"Family" photo of artists and prominent attendees at the art
exhibition at OPEC Fund headquarters (2003)*

It was at this time that I stumbled across the zither, a
musical instrument featured in one of my favorite films, *The
Third Man.* Being a fan of Graham Greene, the screenplay
writer, I had always been enticed by the music in the film. In
keeping with my own personal interest in promoting the arts,
I took the initiative to curate an art exhibition featuring three
artists hailing from diverse parts of the globe. Among them
were a Brazilian, a Kuwaiti, and a Palestinian, each contributing
a unique cultural perspective. The exhibition garnered significant attention, especially when word spread that the Kuwaiti
artist had honed his craft under the mentorship of Kokoshka,
renowned as maestro in the late 1950s. It also served as a platform to showcase the profound talents of these individuals
and was a personal highlight of my time in Austria, though my
focus remained on international affairs.

IAEA

My interest in arms control and disarmament was reignited in Vienna, which houses the headquarters of the International Atomic Energy Agency (IAEA) and the Comprehensive Test Ban Treaty Organization (CTBTO). The 35-member Board of Governors (BOG) of the IAEA is composed of representatives from the thirteen countries most advanced in atomic energy technology and elected officials from member states, who serve for two-year terms. By tradition, the five permanent members of the Security Council do not seek the chairmanship. With some advance preparation, there was the possibility that Kuwait could even assume the chairmanship of the BOG.

A view held at the time was that the state holding the chairmanship had to either be knowledgeable in nuclear technology or engage in nuclear activities. For the Middle East and Southern Asia (MESA) group, only Kuwait, India, Iran, and Saudi Arabia were eligible for the chairmanship for the term 2002–2003. Kuwait touched base with Saudi Arabia to garner their support and sent feelers out to Iran and India, with mixed results. Iran dragged their feet, and India, being non-party to the Non-Proliferation Treaty (NPT) and with its 1994 and 1998 nuclear tests, did little to endear itself to other countries when it came to steering a body like the IAEA.

By contacting colleagues, building support, and gaining invaluable backing from headquarters, Kuwait was selected by consensus as Chairman of the IAEA Board of Governors for 2002–2003. Becoming the first Arab woman and only the third woman at all to hold this position since the establishment of the IAEA in 1957 was a momentous occasion. A sixteen-year gap since the last woman (from Indonesia) chaired the BOG highlighted the rarity of such occurrences. I took the reins and was later heartened by the subsequent appointments of two Arab women, Taous Feroukhi from Algeria in 2008, and Leena Al-Hadid from Jordan in 2018.

My experience as Chairman was rich and grueling. It highlighted the importance of consensus across the board in order to achieve any kind of meaningful decision. Together with my team, we tried to familiarize ourselves with the different departments of the IAEA. I was fortunate and pleased to have the added support of Dr. Jassem Bishara, who was the Head of the Kuwait Institute for Scientific Research (KISR). There was also great input by Kuwaiti colleague Dr. Adnan Shihab-Eldin, who was Director of the Division for Africa, Asia & Far East of the IAEA. My friendship with him and his wife, Bana, an accomplished artist, continues to this day.

During my tenure, colleagues alerted me to the importance of attending to the zero-growth budget of the Agency, which was the norm for quite some time. In justifying a proposed budget increase, I privately commissioned a comprehensive documentation of the conceptual rationale. This documentation highlighted both the current and anticipated surge to meet safeguard activities, underscored by the simultaneous decrease in the availability of resources and qualified workers. Crafting a set of talking points proved invaluable in guiding the démarche. In order to ensure smooth acceptance by individual member states, a phased approach to increasing the budget was suggested. Quite a number of "shielded" states, i.e., states that are granted partial relief for safeguards assessments and are not required to pay the full rate of budget dues, mostly from the G77 and China, would have to meet the higher financial obligations. The active support of Japan and Germany were of great strategic importance in this matter.

One of the most visible aspects of the organization, outside of the political sphere, was the issue of verification of non-proliferation based on the NPT. Three countries, the Democratic People's Republic of Korea (DPRK), Iran, and Iraq all had some arrangement with the IAEA to verify their nuclear programs, and during my tenure all three would quite suddenly leap to the fore.

DPRK

In October 2002, information started to trickle in that the DPRK was embarking on some uranium enrichment activities. This issue had been dormant since 1993, but suddenly multiple attempts by the IAEA and other international players to mediate and solve the crisis came to naught. IAEA inspectors were expelled from North Korea in December 2002. I was completely thrown off and changed my own personal holiday plans to remain in Vienna for the New Year. I held consultations with colleagues and endeavored to meet the inspectors who had just been expelled. They had quite the experience, and upon meeting them, I noted with marvel that one of the inspectors was an Egyptian woman.

One issue that kept on recurring through the DPRK episode was the term "correctness and completeness." This meant that the information received by the IAEA was insufficient to pronounce its satisfaction with the compliance of the concerned party. That phrase would later aptly describe the information supplied by Iran, which evaded full transparency in supplying information.

In early 2003, the Board of Governors voted on a resolution that led the DPRK to unilaterally announce its withdrawal from the NPT, the first time a nation had ever done so. Long discussions ensued, but ultimately the Board decided it was not in a position to pronounce itself on the question of withdrawal. The issue was referred to the Security Council in February 2003, and the question of withdrawal from the NPT would continue to be discussed over the years.

Invasion of Iraq

It was during my time in Austria that I experienced the shock of the September 11 attacks in 2001, the first of two years of our membership in the Board of Governors of the IAEA, which was then chaired by Australia. I learned of the attacks on the twin towers from my brother Lutfi, who was in London transiting to New York. He frantically asked me to watch TV, to which I frustratedly replied that I had none. I had come to our midtown office during a break from the Board's meetings, and the rented embassy offices in Vienna were not equipped at the time with such luxury. Rushing back to the IAEA, we resumed the meeting but used earphones connected to CNN relaying updates. Realizing the gravity of the situation, we quickly wrapped the meeting up and watched the unfolding events on an enlarged screen. Everyone was in shock. We had no words except to comfort Kenneth Brill, our American colleague. Later that afternoon and the following day, I touched base with friends and colleagues in New York to ensure their safety. The shock remained with us, and we had but words condemning the terrorist attack.

The IAEA and the BOG received widespread coverage and media attention leading up to the invasion of Iraq. Discussions taking place between the United Nations Monitoring and Verification Commission (UNMOVIC) and Iraqi authorities in Vienna during the summer of 2002 earned the Agency the crude title of "watchdog." It was a moniker that we would be unable to shake, as it was used for a variety of issues. The IAEA was kept informed on two aspects of its program—the safeguards agreement with the Agency, and activities mandated by the UNSC.

All eyes were on Vienna as the Bush Administration pushed the theory that weapons of mass destruction were being produced within Iraq. In mid-March 2003, the Board of Governors was breaking news to the world that the inspectors in Iraq were to be withdrawn for safety reasons, following advice from the Director-General Dr. Mohamed ElBaradei of Egypt. Kenneth Brill, our American colleague, preferred to delay the announcement until something came out of New York rather than Vienna. However, I agreed with the DG that it should not be postponed and I approved an open session—a rare occurrence, as meetings are normally closed to the public. The session, as expected, was abuzz with media. Drawn to his congenial but firm style of leadership, I worked well with Dr. ElBaradei and deferred to his consul.

There was a general feeling that the US was more interested in getting rid of Saddam Hussein, and I firmly believe that more time should have been given to the inspectors to confirm the absence of weapons of mass destruction. I commended the speeches of the Director-General and that of Hans Blix to the Security Council, both of which emphasized the need for more time—a view that was not widely shared by others.

With Dr. Mohamed ElBaradei, Director-General of the International Atomic Energy Agency (IAEA) (2003)

A major concern for the Agency was the security of Tuwaitha Nuclear Research Center, where nuclear material, specifically yellow cake, was supposedly sealed off. In the rush to take Baghdad, the Tuwaitha facility was not secured. Contents were looted for scrap lead, which led to widespread contamination. The Agency pressed our American colleague to intercede with authorities in order to secure the site. Meanwhile, the Iraqi opposition in Vienna approached me to air their concerns about local Iraqis who were misusing seized barrels for personal storage and had suffered chemical burns. In a July 2003 report, the Director-General wrote, "the quantity and type of uranium compounds dispersed are not sensitive from a proliferation point of view," but they were hazardous to health. In response to these claims, the Agency requested access to the site from the Americans; however, it took until the middle of June 2003 to get the inspectors back to Tuwaitha, and only with the assistance of Kuwait to facilitate their passage without fanfare.

Another unfortunate incident that occurred in August 2003 was the terrorist attack at the UN Headquarters in Baghdad, which targeted the UN Assistance Mission for Iraq (UNAMI). My office staff in Vienna broke the news to me in between meetings. I was shaken by the untimely deaths of a good friend and UN official Nadia Younis and her boss, Sergio de Mello, UN Special Representative for Iraq, as well as the serious injury of a family friend, Nada Nashef. Thankfully, Nada would make a full recovery and continue to work with the United Nations.

On 1 May 2003, President Bush appeared on the deck of the USS *Abraham Lincoln*, off the coast of San Diego, and declared: "Mission accomplished." I did not believe that the mission was complete, and I recall ruefully commenting to an American colleague that this was a great photo opportunity. He was not amused.

The Iranian Syndrome

One cannot separate Iran from any issue in the Gulf, as the Iranian presence pervades the region. While this may not seem the case to outsiders, this is a fact deeply ingrained in all those who reside in the Arabian Peninsula. The Iranian nuclear program was revealed to the world in August 2002. This was followed in September by a statement by the Vice President and Head of the Atomic Energy Organization of Iran, in which he stressed the importance of abiding by international treaties, including the Non-Proliferation Treaty, and the need for Iran to embark on an energy mix. His statement also alluded to attempts to strike a balance between the promotion and verification of activities of the IAEA. I regarded this statement as little more than political posturing and was concerned, among others, about Iran's nuclear program.

The first time I personally encountered any sort of posturing around the question of Iran's nuclear program was when my Iranian colleague confided in me that he was taken aback with the Agency's demand for information on its nuclear facilities. Needless to say, I prompted him to take that demand seriously if the country had nothing to conceal and was pursuing a peaceful nuclear program. As we were both graduates of AUB, we had a good working relationship. He spoke fluent Arabic and would find excuses to come to my office to indulge in some Arabic coffee and conversation. I also endeared myself to certain members of the BOG by taking small pauses to break fasting during Ramadan, a gesture that was appreciated by the Muslim representatives.

The first IAEA report on the nuclear program of Iran was in March 2003, against the backdrop of the Iraq war and the DPRK issue. The Iranians were savvy when dealing with the West, indeed with all, a trait others did not possess. Members of the Board raised the issue, requesting that the Director-General report on nuclear activity in Iran. The DG appealed for transparency on the part of Iran and requested cooperation without invoking specific articles of a safeguard agreement. Unlike the DPRK, where there was little or no dialogue with the Agency, there were always indications from the Iranian government that they were willing to cooperate. Iran was a member of BOG in 2003. Indeed, there was direct communication between the E3 (UK, France, Germany) because they feared getting embroiled in another conflict in the region and were keen to avoid that scenario. Outside of the IAEA, the Iranians submitted a proposal in May 2003 that included:

1) Transparency on the Iran nuclear program
2) Cooperation to stabilize Iraq
3) Access to peaceful nuclear technology
4) Acceptance of the Arab League's 2002 "Land for Peace" initiative
5) Removal of US sanctions

This proposal was immediately dismissed by the US administration in favor of additional pressure on the Iranian authorities. While a majority of nations sought dialogue and diplomacy to solve this issue, the US administration pushed a more aggressive track. The first pronouncements by the BOG occurred on 19 June 2003, and they urged Iran to cooperate. This was the thrust of a statement I delivered at the time. (See Annex for this statement.)

Many countries, particularly the non-aligned, viewed the Iranian issue with skepticism, and for the first time formed into a group in the IAEA. A majority of members did not think that the issue merited a quick referral to the Security Council. As a Kuwaiti, I was sensitive to the fact that such a move should not happen under my chairmanship. The Europeans were keen to find a solution through dialogue and came together in the late spring of 2003. The E3 put forth a joint proposal to prevent escalation, hoping to avert a scenario like the contentious invasion of Iraq. Consultation was deemed necessary to press for a diplomatic solution. All through this period, the Gulf States were following developments with interest. We were spectators keen to see how the issue would evolve or be resolved. At the same time, this issue sparked an interest in nuclear energy in the region.

The international demand for greater openness on the part of Iran continued to be a thorny issue, with a majority of states wavering or trying to balance the legitimate pursuit of a peaceful nuclear program with compliance with safeguards arrangements by the Agency. Normally, the Agency concludes agreements with all states, some more robust than others, the optimum one being party to the Additional Protocol of 1997, which provides additional tools for verification of peaceful uses of nuclear material. The Additional Protocol for verification of nuclear safeguards came about following the realization that regular agreements with the DPRK were insufficient to detect undeclared nuclear material. It was criticized by some states for its intrusiveness, or for not being equally demanding of countries with sizable nuclear programs. Kuwait was supportive of robust verification, and I personally deposited the instruments of ratification to the Additional Protocol in 2003.

Departing the Habsburg Capital

While not as prominent as the challenges posed by the crises in DPRK, Iran, or Iraq, another noteworthy issue arose in the form of the procedural intricacies surrounding the annual report submission to the United Nations General Assembly (UNGA). The process of streamlining these reports, initially sanctioned by the BOG, encountered a hurdle, as there were attempts to introduce amendments in New York that were not accepted during the preparation of the report in Vienna. To prevent any potential unraveling of the report and to facilitate a smoother passage, deliberate efforts were undertaken. This strategic approach aimed to mitigate confrontations among the broader membership of the United Nations, ensuring that the Agency's reports navigated through the complexities of international discourse with greater ease.

In early 2002, following multiple requests from the concerned public, the government of Kuwait requested the assistance of the IAEA in determining the possible long-term radiological impacts of depleted uranium munitions. It was the first time that an international group was created in order to study depleted uranium. A consortium including British and South African experts, IAEA officials, the United Nations

Environment Programme (UNEP), and the World Health Organization (WHO) were sent to eleven different locations in Kuwait to test for potential radiation contamination. In Vienna, we had to facilitate the transport and release of around 200 environmental samples to their destinations. The IAEA investigation concluded that depleted uranium does not pose a radiological hazard to the people of Kuwait. The report was the first comprehensive radiological assessment of compliance with international radiation criteria.[4]

A part of my time in Vienna was dedicated to the Test Ban Treaty Organization (TBTO). Despite Kuwait's non-nuclear status, we hosted a radionuclide station that was active and indeed detected the Chernobyl accident before the station was formalized by the TBTO. Advocating for Kuwait's ratification of the Treaty, I personally deposited our instruments of ratification in May 2003, convinced of the aggregate value by general membership to such arms control instruments. Unfortunately, regional constraints involving Iran and Israel limited our active participation in the organization's workings.

Towards the end of my tenure in Vienna, a colleague brought up an issue that struck a chord with me. She spoke of a sense of "deflation" and potential marginalization following the end of a high-ranking position. This got me thinking about my own future and whether it was time for a change of environment, despite my overall contentment with my posting in Vienna. I was shaken out of that mood by Sheikh Dr. Mohammad Sabah Al-Salem Al-Sabah, Minister of Foreign

---

4 https://www.iaea.org/newscenter/news/depleted-uranium-kuwait

Affairs of the State of Kuwait, as I was returning from a trip to Slovakia. During our conversation, he revealed that he was proposing me as the Permanent Representative to the United Nations, catching me completely off guard. Despite privately knowing that my name had not been included in an earlier shortlist for the position, I was deeply touched by his unexpected gesture. I requested time to think it over, which was most definitely not how this was done normally. Serving at the UN in New York is a highly coveted opportunity for diplomats, and I said yes. The announcement of my appointment came in September 2003. However, due to bureaucratic delays, I would not assume the post until January 2004.

Caricature presented to me by Ambassador Ken Brill at the end of my tenure as Chairman of the Board of Governors of the IAEA, Vienna, Austria (2003)

If I were to rate Vienna as a posting, I would state that it is a prime one. It combines both high quality of life and professional satisfaction. I must admit that my view may be partially biased due to a remarkable engagement at the time as Chairman of the Board of Governors from 2002–2003. As I bid farewell, I was contacted by Austrian officials who informed me that in recognition of my work as Ambassador to Austria, they were bestowing upon me a decoration. In 2004 I was presented with the Austrian Grand Golden Decoration of Honor for First Class Merit by my Austrian colleague in New York.

Ambassador Gerhard Pfanzelter, Permanent Representative of Austria to the United Nations, presenting me with the Austrian Grand Golden Decoration of Honor for First Class Merit (2004)

Back to the UN, Jewel in the Crown

The love of one's country is a splendid thing.
But why should love stop at the border?
—Pablo Casals

Assignment to be Permanent Representative to the UN is considered to be the crown jewel of one's career in diplomacy. My designation as Permanent Representative in 2004 was greeted with interest, as it was the first instance of an Arab woman heading a member state's delegation. I confided to a close colleague that I was sanguine about this opportunity. The public often fixated on the prestige of the UN position, neglecting my impactful contributions at the IAEA, however. In later years, I felt that the role seemed to cast a shadow on my prior term as Chairman of the Board at the IAEA, an unfairly overlooked accomplishment.

Professionally it would be an extremely rewarding time. On a personal level, it offered me the chance to reconnect with friends, yet it was also a traumatic and grueling time. A friend once advised me that it was best not to be reassigned to a former post. There were eight women Permanent Representatives when I presented my credentials. By the time I was relocated to Belgium, the total had increased to around thirty, primarily from the Caribbean, Eastern Europe, and Africa. My Egyptian colleague, whom I knew from my earlier assignment at the UN, profusely commended Kuwait for the appointment. My immediate response was that Kuwait was a latecomer to UN membership, only joining in 1963, whilst Egypt was a signatory member since 1945. Yet Egypt had quite a number of women ambassadors around the world. Eventually quite a number of Arab women were at the helm, but not during my posting.

The presentation of my credentials to Kofi Annan, the Secretary-General at the time, was a pleasant occasion. During the private chat, we reminisced about past experiences when he was Head of Personnel, and later, Peacekeeping Operations. The US Permanent Representative, John Negroponte, was in the corridor at the time and greeted me warmly.

Presentation of my credentials to United Nations Secretary-General Kofi Annan, New York (2004)

Upon the first week of my arrival, I was thrust into the responsibility of presenting the country report of Kuwait to the Convention on the Elimination of All Forms of Discrimination Against Women (CEDAW). I was expecting a team of professionals from Kuwait to oversee the task; however, the delegation's travel was delayed due to visa issues. Hastily, I tapped two capable Kuwaiti women posted to non-political functions in Washington to assist. Our report went smoothly, and members of the Committee lauded having a female Permanent Representative in New York.

Another unforeseen task that I was handed as soon as I began my tenure was the early preparation for a conference in Kuwait for Friends of Iraq. It would be the first time that the new Iraqi government participated in gatherings since the US invasion of the country in 2003. I was instructed to check with the Iraqi Foreign Minister, Hoshyar Zebari, who at the time was in New York, about the appropriate date. Kuwait's outreach to Iraq was of great importance, with the rationale of encouraging Iraq back into the fold instead of ostracizing it.

With Sheikh Dr. Mohammad Sabah Al-Salem Al-Sabah, Minister of Foreign Affairs of the State of Kuwait, at the Friends of Iraq meeting in Kuwait City (2004)

Participating in the meeting in March 2004 in Kuwait was enriching. Upon my return to New York, I found that I had inadvertently obtained a high profile in the midst of more experienced colleagues and set the path for closer interaction with the UN Representative to Iraq, the veteran Algerian diplomat

Lakhdar Ibrahimi Brahimi. He had a congenial demeanor and was willing to impart insights from his missions to occupied Iraq as the Representative of the Secretary-General. One particularly memorable occasion was a working lunch I hosted for close associates at my residence, where an unexpected encounter with Jalal Talabani, member of the Iraqi Governing Council and later President in 2005, delayed him. I decided to be bold and extended the invitation to him as well. In response to my customary greeting, saying, "You are welcome, the house is yours," a jovial Talabani retorted that he had no intention of replicating Saddam Hussein in his occupation of Kuwait!

The Greater Middle East Initiative, launched in 2004, also captured our attention, aiming to transform the region toward greater democracy and human development. I accompanied the Foreign Minister at the inaugural meeting held in the impressive grand hall of the Waldorf Astoria New York in the presence of an array of foreign ministers. The initiative was originally that of a G-8 Summit and was viewed with skepticism in the region and elsewhere. There was no genuine partnership at the drawing board. Under my breath, I whispered to the Foreign Minister that it seemed there was a creation of unnecessary new mechanisms to get the initiative rolling instead of borrowing a wheel that was there.

One of the most pleasant moments during my diplomatic journey was overseeing Kuwait's hosting the annual UN Day in October 2004. After stiff competition from other nations to host the event at the prestigious General Assembly Hall, this marked a significant milestone, as it was the first time an Arab member state had the privilege. The occasion served as a platform to showcase Kuwait's rich musical and artistic heritage. I offered a talented Kuwaiti artist, Bana, the opportunity to showcase her work during the national day reception. While the groundwork and meticulous pre-planning had been laid before my move to New York, the execution of the event became my responsibility. I seized the opportunity to introduce the Kuwaiti National Orchestra and Kuwaiti Television Band at the UN. Following the performance, I hosted a reception where I presented the Secretary-General with a showpiece—an elaborate model of the UN House in Kuwait. This was a tangible representation of my government's plan to donate a headquarters in Kuwait to the United Nations, a source of pride for Kuwait as it continued to support and facilitate the missions of the UN.

Among the different portfolios a Kuwaiti representative holds is the Chairmanship of the Islamic Cultural Center in New York, a project initiated by numerous Muslim states, with Kuwait being the prime financial donor. Indeed, it was Sheikh Jaber Al-Ahmad Al-Sabah in his capacity as Chairman of the Organization of Islamic Conference (OIC, and renamed the Organization of Islamic Cooperation in 2011) who broke ground for the mosque at the center in 1988. It was an interesting experience with almost an all-male Board of Trustees. I opted for a low-key, business-as-usual attitude in such a delicate circumstance.

Kuwait hosting the annual United Nations Day, New York (2004)

Presenting a model of the United Nations House in Kuwait to UN Secretary-General Kofi Annan and his wife (at right), New York (2004)

In 2005 the United Nations ventured into the realm of cinema, allowing the shooting of a film called *The Interpreter,* starring Nicole Kidman. The annual luncheon hosted by Secretary-General Kofi Annan for delegates witnessed the excitement of ambassadors, with one even volunteering to play a role as a delegate, showcasing the magnetic allure of celebrities in diplomatic circles. The filming coincided with greater reach by the UN into civil society, while also being an immensely fun experience.

In another such instance in 2015, the UN brought Colombian singer Shakira, of Lebanese roots, to the General Assembly Hall to sing "Imagine." I took pride in referring to her as an example of a celebrity actively promoting international norms and engaging in civil society causes.

Shortly after my arrival in New York, my team became preoccupied with preparations for the visit of His Highness the Amir Sheikh Jaber Al-Ahmad Al-Sabah for medical treatment. It was a difficult time, managing the expected workload along with the increased traffic of visitors. One relief was the presence of my sister, who was visiting at the time. I felt blessed to be able to have my family around me during these demanding moments. Fortunately, His Highness's condition improved, which was a major relief to all. I personally held him in such high esteem. My initial swearing-in ceremony as Ambassador was in his presence, and I had the privilege of being granted an audience with him when I touched base at home.

I had the opportunity to bond with other women ambassadors due to our American colleague who organized a trip for us to visit New Orleans in April 2005. The governor of Louisiana at the time was a woman, and we were invited for a meeting at the Chamber of Commerce. One of the invitees was the legendary jazz musician Wynton Marsalis. It was my first time in New Orleans, and I could not leave without experiencing Mardi Gras. Shortly after our trip, Hurricane Katrina struck and I was involved in arranging Kuwait's contribution to the US relief and rescue efforts.

Meanwhile, the entire UN was abuzz with preparation for the UN World Summit 2005. One of the major topics of the Agenda for Peace, which was laboriously negotiated in 2005 at the UN World Summit, was the "Responsibility to Protect" or R2P. It is an international principle that seeks to ensure that the international community never again fails to halt the mass atrocity crimes of genocide, war crimes, ethnic cleansing, and crimes against humanity. Paragraph 138 of the World Summit Outcome Document states:

> Each individual State has the responsibility to protect its populations from genocide, war crimes, ethnic cleansing, and crimes against humanity. This responsibility entails the prevention of such crimes, including their incitement, through appropriate and necessary means. We accept that responsibility and will act in accordance with it. The international community should, as appropriate, encourage and help States to exercise this responsibility and support the United Nations in establishing an early warning capability.

While disarmament loomed on the horizon, it was the issues of R2P that proved to be intractable. The idea of R2P, specifically addressed in 2005, was not a novelty. I believe that it was the underlying rationale for Lifeline Sudan in 1989, a project in coordination with Sudan to alleviate the humanitarian crisis in the southern part of the country at the time. It was also the rationale for the establishment of a no-fly zone over northern Iraq by the coalition against Iraq in 1991, to protect the Kurdish enclave. The turning point for the principle came with the 1994 Rwanda genocide and the 1995 Srebrenica genocide, in the former Yugoslavia.

In April 2006 the UNSC reaffirmed the principle of R2P, lending it an air of mystique that remained pervasive during its discussions. I felt that there was a persistent misunderstanding surrounding the stance of Non-Aligned countries, with some

Western observers erroneously claiming the non-aligned countries' supposed opposition to the principle. This misconception did not sit well with me, and I endeavored to set the record straight. As a matter of fact, Kuwait, Jordan, and Singapore were among those in support of incorporating the R2P principle into the discourse back in 2005. It is a disconcerting display of arrogance when Western officials assume that their narrative will prevail on the global stage, an issue that would crop up consistently in my career.

The principle was revisited in March 2011 when the Security Council authorized military intervention in Libya. It was the first case explicitly citing R2P, and a NATO-led alliance conducted air strikes against military targets that posed a severe threat to civilians. Since Libya, there have been other crises to which the principle of R2P could apply, including, but not limited to, those in the Central African Republic, Syria, Burundi, and Yemen. However, the political will was missing.

My time at the United Nations coincided with some of the more controversial issues with Iraq, primarily maintaining the security of the border that had been demarcated by international teams and affirmed in SC Resolution 833 (1993). The issue at hand was the maintenance of the pillar posts along the demarcated international boundary, which was supposed to be financed by both Iraq and Kuwait. There was also the issue of the continued encroachment by Iraqis who were pressured into farming on Kuwaiti territory.

Eventually, Kuwait decided to officially request that the UN look into the issue. I was well-prepared with satellite images and an official letter that needed to be hand-delivered to the

United Nations. As I awaited the appointment, I received a call from my brother's household in Long Island that he had failed to wake up. I was in utter shock at the news of his death, as I had expected to have dinner with him in a few days. I handed Kuwait's official letter to the secretariat and proceeded to my brother's home, making sure to inform the rest of the family. My own shock and grief were somewhat tempered by my thoughts of the effect on the family, and especially my mother. She had already gone through the trauma of losing a husband, two brothers, and now a second son.

News travels fast. Colleagues offered help while I was en route to his home, and friends comforted me during the following twenty-four hours. I had to make arrangements to fly back home with my brother's coffin the following day. After observing an initial period of condolences in Kuwait, officials requested me to board a flight to Cleveland, Ohio, where the Amir was undergoing medical treatment. I departed with the blessing of my mother.

I found that the return to mundane work and activities served to mitigate the pain I felt from losing my brother. I resumed my duties and functions, which included presenting my credentials to the Bahamas as Ambassador. I proceeded with a false sense of confidence, due to my previous experience presenting credentials and, as shared earlier, I did not pay attention to the fine print in their protocol's guidebook. That was a mistake! Upon arrival to Nassau, it dawned on me that the required attire was quite formal, meaning a dress rather than a pantsuit, and a hat was also required, as was the case in South Africa immediately after the end of apartheid. I had to make haste and find a suitable garment, and I reminded myself not to fall into the trap of overconfidence again.

I was received by the Governor-General Dame Ivy Dumont, the first time the Bahamas had a woman at the helm. She surprised me with her genuine awe that Kuwait had a woman ambassador, a recurring theme in my career, and she presented me with the gift of a book on the Bahamas. On my part, I commended her on being the first woman to assume the post of Governor-General, and knowing that she had an academic background, I gifted her with a pen from the American University of Kuwait, a university that I was initially associated with on their Board of Trustees.

Presentation of my credentials to the Governor-General of the Bahamas, Dame Ivy Dumont (2005)

135

Back in New York, the follow-up work of the General Assembly kept me too busy to dwell on personal concerns, until I learned of the Amir's passing. Together with my colleagues at the office, we made arrangements for condolences, including the memorial service at the GA. All of us were greatly touched by the gesture of the President of the GA at the time, Jan Eliasson of Sweden, who requested that we reschedule the memorial until he could be there in person, as he wanted to preside over the meeting in lieu of a Vice President. This was highly appreciated by all and, in a way, not surprising. Kuwait has worked very closely with Eliasson throughout the years, dating back to when he was responsible for humanitarian affairs at the UN in the 1990s.

Part of my duties, as in all diplomatic posts, was to receive delegations from the National Assembly of Kuwait. On one such occasion, the Speaker at the time, Jassem Al-Kharafi, arrived as part of a meeting of the Inter-Parliamentary Union (IPU) at the UN General Assembly. I was of the mind that the relationship between the IPU and the UN should remain informal given the varied political nuances among parliaments of the world.

I would receive the Speaker Al-Kharafi in multiple cities, in different postings throughout my career. I was struck by his strength of character and generosity. In Vienna, he intervened to personally cover the medical expenses of a Kuwaiti national. In New York, he provided financial backing to host Iftar at the Islamic Center. I would encounter him again in Brussels, where my contacts in Namibia would prove useful. He would seek my advice when dealing with Theo-Ben Gurirab, then President of the IPU. I had worked closely with Ben Gurirab during his time as prime minister of Namibia, and we had become close friends.

If I had any qualms about my return to working in New York, it was reinforced by the personal challenges I went through as I grieved my brother's death. Eventually, I was relocated to Belgium. In between those assignments, I was invited along with other women from the region by St. Antony's College of Oxford University to address the question of women in diplomacy. Each of us addressed a corresponding field of the recently published UN *Arab Human Development Report,* which had been prepared by academics and officials from the region. I recall the abrupt manner in which it was presented to the Arab ambassadors at the UN. Few of us knew about it in the making. We were completely disconnected due to a lack of communication and networking in official sectors. Such circumstances often lead to misconceptions between the UN Secretariat and representatives, as was the case with the presentation of this report.

To the Heart of Europe

Never let your sense of morals get in the way of doing what's right.

—Isaac Asimov

Belgium is a beautiful but odd place, with a mix of different cultures and languages that vary even between neighboring cities. It was here, in Brussels, that I would make my final stop on my tour as a diplomat.

It is the norm that one has to be accredited to the primary host, in this case the King of the Belgians, and then follow up with the other postings and institutions in the country. Like Austria, Belgium was host to a number of organizations that included the European Union and the North Atlantic Treaty Organization. Though I was not yet accredited to the European Union, I decided that I should attend the annual reception hosted by the President of the European Parliament, Hans-Gert Pöttering. Some colleagues might have delegated other staff to attend such a function, but I thought of myself as the "flag" or representative of Kuwait and felt I should always honor invitations and show a presence at official functions as a principal duty, reflecting courtesy and interest to hosts. I wanted to be seen and engaged.

As I was ushered into the welcoming line, the President expressed surprise at the fact that I was a woman, proving once again that perceptions matter. I was dismayed. I became acutely aware of a similar reaction from an Austrian journalist, who also marveled at the thought of a female Kuwaiti ambassador. I retorted that I congratulated Austria for appointing the first woman in its history to the post of Minister for Foreign Affairs.

There were quite a number of women Heads of Mission. At NATO, however, only the US, followed by France, had a female ambassador. As in Austria, I enjoyed the friendship of the dean of the women's corps, the Ambassador of the Philippines. I also befriended Ambassador Leila Shahid of Palestine, who displayed exemplary dedication and proficiency in a milieu that was often unresponsive to the Palestinian cause. Eventually, Egypt, as well as the GCC, were also represented by women. Ambassador Amal Al-Hamad, a skilled diplomat, was an invaluable sounding board, and we have remained close friends ever since.

Meeting the president of the European Parliament, Brussels, Belgium (2007)

Presenting my credentials to His Majesty King Albert II, King of the Belgians, Brussels, Belgium (2007)

With Ambassador Amal Al-Hamad (right) at a reception in Brussels, Belgium (2007)

European Union

Upon my arrival in Brussels, a diplomatic challenge presented itself as I learned that the Kuwaiti Prime Minister, accompanied by a sizable delegation, was set to visit in December 2007 at the invitation of the European Union. Faced with a residence undergoing repairs, my sister and I had to creatively improvise with available space to accommodate the visiting group for lunch.

Another early challenge of great impact that I faced in Brussels was a subtle attempt by the European Commission to streamline sovereign funds by adopting a code of conduct without first consulting us, or others, as to where the funds were based. The European draft was intended for adoption by the IMF or World Bank to control foreign inflow in strategic industries. If it were to become an international instrument without our input, it could adversely impact Kuwait's investments in Europe. I came across this draft by accident when I stumbled upon a related document that was not widely circulated. I hastened to inform officials back home, in particular our investment institutions. Luckily the matter was attended to, and my role ended there. Shortly thereafter, countries endowed with sovereign funds did come together to establish an institution of their own. The International Working Group of Sovereign Wealth Funds was primarily a consultative body whose main purpose was to meet, exchange views, and facilitate an understanding of generally accepted principles and practices.

On this theme of European centrism was another attempt by the EU to implement a carbon tax for aviation fuel. As they tried to rally support for this endeavor, I responded that any carbon tax scheme should not be not the initiative of a regional bloc, but should come from the International Civil Aviation Organization. They eventually opted to introduce a carbon tax only for flights to and from the EU.

These episodes, among other instances, reinforced my belief that the Western world was prone to rushing into things, adopting regulations and practices that turned out to be skewed. To back up this perception, I often cited American economist Alan Greenspan, who, following the 2008 financial meltdown, famously acknowledged during his testimony to

Congress that he was wrong in opposing regulations.

Another instance that demanded attention was the European Union's démarches at the United Nations. It was the practice to prepare drafts, which are difficult to amend, given that they were the result of consensus. My reaction to my European colleagues was that representatives of other states in Brussels needed to be consulted to make the passage of drafts easier in other fora. That advice was not heeded. The argument that the EU often makes is that the text is an outcome of lengthy negotiations that will be hard to alter.

Interactions with the European Union were of great and varied importance. On the bilateral level, Kuwait engaged with the EU with the aim of attaining visa-free travel for its nationals within the Schengen Area. This initiative would remain stalled for years as Kuwait and the EU exchanged many high-level delegations on a wide range of topics, attempting to boost relations and attain a breakthrough. I regularly attended the EU's Delegation for Relations with the Arab Peninsula (DARP) meetings at the European Parliament, where I never shied away from the opportunity to show that Kuwait was more than willing to engage with its European partners in an open and frank manner.

In addition to engaging with the EU bilaterally, Kuwait did so on the multilateral track through the Gulf Cooperation Council (GCC). The GCC–EU relationship is based on a 1989 Cooperation Agreement, which established regular dialogue and cooperation between both sides in a wide number of fields.

These annual GCC–EU Joint Council and Ministerial Meetings would alternate between the GCC countries currently holding the presidency of the organization and the EU headquarters in Brussels or Luxembourg. As part of the GCC delegation in Brussels and Luxembourg, I actively participated in the negotiations over the final draft of the meeting—and had direct responsibility during the one in Luxembourg in 2010. Kuwait ended up coordinating ministerial meetings twice during my tenure when Kuwait held the GCC presidency. Facilitating this complex task was the invaluable contribution of the GCC Mission to Brussels, under the leadership of Ambassador Amal.

At a meeting of the Delegation for Relations with the Arab Peninsula (DARP) at the European Parliament in Brussels, Belgium (2010)

These meetings expanded to include negotiations on concluding a free-trade agreement, which each side recognized as being important. However, major challenges emerged, ranging from templates proposed by the European side to the difficulty in finding common ground or mutually agreed-upon language in the texts. Despite these hurdles, the experience of participating in meetings proved to be invaluable and fascinating. Eventually, both sides resorted to much shorter final statements on the meetings.

Arab Spring

One of the more interesting international developments during my time in Brussels was the advent of what those in the West called the "Arab Spring." From the start, I was uneasy with that label being used to describe the changes in the Middle East. It was a term borrowed by the West to describe the early 1990s in Eastern Europe and hastily ascribed to the Arab world. I argued with colleagues that the repurposing of this term seemed to indicate a mental lethargy in trying to address the changes on a case-by-case basis. The revolts that swept through the region were not unprecedented, after all. Their significance lay in the unraveling of states from within, a testament to the failure of institutions to adapt to an increasingly open society and aspiring youth.

My direct experience with the Arab Spring was in late December 2010, with the imminent collapse of the government in Tunisia. At the time, I held the Chairmanship of the Arab Group among the accredited ambassadors in Brussels.

My Tunisian colleague was facing mounting difficulties within his embassy, and he eventually sought sanctuary in Belgium, which was granted by the authorities. Witnessing the plight of fellow career diplomats who faced these uncertainties evoked feelings of sympathy. As the "Jasmine Revolution" (another name for the era) accelerated and intensified, the EU decided to hold a meeting to chart the way forward for the new authorities in Tunisia. Including Kuwait, some Arab countries were invited, and I was astounded by the detailed roadmap the EU presented, fearing that it might overwhelm the nascent Tunisian leadership. In the absence of any specific instructions, my intervention was motivated by a sense of Arab solidarity with Tunisia. I spoke publicly and said that if there were more letters in the alphabet, the EU would add them to the list of the roadmap that Tunisia was required to comply with. To my surprise, a senior EU official privately expressed appreciation for my input.

In early 2011, Egypt also found itself at the center of a tumultuous turn of events. I received a tip from a close media contact that Catherine Ashton, the High Representative of the European Union for Foreign Affairs and Security Policy, was poised to attach EU support to the protesters in Tahrir Square against the Egyptian government. In response, I immediately contacted my Egyptian colleague to alert her to the shifting sentiments within EU circles. There was palpable wariness regarding official Western support for the demonstrations.

The turn of events in Libya brought another unique challenge to our diplomatic efforts. Guided by a collective position within the GCC, the Arab League reached out to the

UN Security Council as the Libyan leader's brutal crackdown on the opposition drew global condemnation. The task of confronting Libya's civil war fell to NATO, which justified its actions based on UNSC resolutions. While a handful of Arab countries joined NATO operations, Kuwait limited its involvement to providing humanitarian assistance to Libya, primarily through the border with Egypt.

The Syrian rebellion of March 2011 was another startling development that prompted the European Union to consult separately with member states. Ambassadors from the GCC countries were invited to provide initial reactions to a rehabilitation plan for Syria, by means of yet another Western template. While we remained non-committal, we stressed the importance of prioritizing issues like water and medical assistance over concepts like women's empowerment and judicial reform. This drew the attention of our hosts, who seemed slightly taken aback that we were not standing fully behind their initiative. Again it seemed that Europeans believed that their templates for dealing with issues should be applied wherever and however they saw fit. Syria's suspension from the Arab League also had significant implications, particularly during the Arab Group meetings in Brussels. The decision came at a delicate moment, on the eve of a meeting that I scheduled. Privately, I coordinated with my Syrian colleague, and he agreed to absent himself, reassured that no decision regarding Syria would be made in his absence, as that was the domain of the League of Arab States. This episode underscored the camaraderie among ambassadors, evident also in our quiet expression of support amid physical threats on the Syrian diplomatic premises, which I conveyed to the Belgian authorities. I was interviewed on this subject, and the article is included in the Annex.

Iran

During my time in Brussels, Iran leapt back into the foray, following diplomatic attempts to bring an end to Tehran's nuclear ambitions. Initially, the EU3 began talks with Iran. The rationale for their interest was to avert a similar crisis that had led to the 2003 war in Iraq and strained relations with the US.

Eventually, in 2006, the American administration shifted its approach from being a passive observer of these talks and began to engage with Iran through discrete diplomatic back-channels. Unbeknown at the time, was the role played by Oman as the venue for these engagements.

Relations were strained due to continued Iranian uranium enrichment operations, and Iran's failure to report on activities related to its program led to the coalescing of other players, the UN Permanent 5 Members + Germany (P5+1 or EU3+3) in June 2006.

Of interest to Kuwait and my GCC colleagues were the insights gained from EU briefings following sessions of the talks with Iran. It was important input for our capitals. From the start, the GCC countries treated the issue as one between Iran and the international community and chose to distance themselves from direct involvement with the talks.

One issue on which all countries, including Iran, agree is the right to the peaceful use of nuclear energy. A key aspect of this is the availability of nuclear fuel, which Iran insists on obtaining independently. In contrast, Kuwait is more than willing to support efforts like those of US Senator Sam Nunn and the Nuclear Threat Initiative (NTI) think-tank in establishing a nuclear fuel bank. This initiative provided an opportunity for countries to obtain low-enriched uranium for use in nuclear reactors. Kuwait's $10 million contribution was the final pledge that sealed the deal to open the bank, a fact I was happy to share with my European colleagues.

NATO

NATO was the awesome military bloc supporting the Atlantic Alliance after World War II and acting as the guardian of Western and liberal values. It was unable to acquire a friendlier perception in the outside world in the 1980s and 1990s, remaining aloof and distant, even after the breakup of the Soviet Union and Warsaw Pact countries. My first glimpse of a softer NATO was when it was outsourced in 2005 by the UN to address a devastating earthquake that affected Pakistan, India, and Afghanistan. At the time, the Norwegian Head of the Office for the Coordination of Humanitarian Affairs at the UN (OCHA) was instrumental in paving the way for NATO's role in the rescue efforts.

In 2008 NATO and the UN concluded an MoU, or framework agreement, for further collaboration. It was not highly publicized due to reluctance by some non-aligned members to disclose the growing relationship between the two institutions. NATO was still supposed to be a "hard" militaristic institution, and Yugoslavia's experience was still fresh in the minds of the international community.

I eventually came to appreciate NATO's coordination efforts in October 1990 when Iraq occupied Kuwait. Secretary of State James Baker addressed the North Atlantic Council (NAC) in September of that year on coordinating military planning while I was engaged with our mission in New York. It was only later in the day that I found out about his address because I had been delving into the position of other organizations on the occupation of Kuwait. In a way, Kuwait and NATO go back to that period, working together long before Kuwait became a NATO partner in 2004 under the Istanbul Cooperation Initiative (ICI).

The basic ICI document refers to general values and other principles that we members of ICI did not take part in inscribing. However, the general thrust of the Initiative as a partnership was a welcome step. There was an attempt in 2012 to revisit the original document of ICI, but I believe there was a decision against that for fear that the basic document would be unraveled. Members of the Mediterranean Dialogue partnership, which include some Arab countries, primarily North African in addition to Jordan and Israel, have no reference document. Political constraints were also a prime consideration to dismiss a floating proposal to inscribe the partnership in a document. There were subtle attempts to merge members of the two partnerships, but they were met with skepticism, if not outright refusal, the rationale being the difference in the security challenges that were met by each with NATO.

And so, my perception of NATO was molded over the

years such that by the time I assumed my post in Brussels, I found myself arguing with colleagues over the negative image of the organization. It was a two-way dilemma, not assisted by NATO's opaqueness. NATO's public diplomacy was yet to evolve efficiently. I became directly involved with NATO beginning in December 2006 as I awaited my transfer from New York to Belgium. My predecessor in Brussels was deep into organizing the first NAC meeting in Kuwait, which is a highlight of the relationship with a partner country. Kuwait was the first GCC country to join NATO's Istanbul Cooperation Initiative in 2004. The Minister of Foreign Affairs at the time assigned me to conduct one official session of that memorable meeting. It made my landing smooth with the NATO members when I later took up my post in Brussels.

Once there, I made my rounds of courtesy calls to the Secretary-General and some other members. I was taken by surprise one day when I received a call from the Deputy Secretary-General Alessandro Minuto Rizzo, who wished to call on me. I thought it was my duty to call on him! I was touched by the gesture, which endeared him to me. It reminded me of the gesture by the Egyptian Ambassador in New York, Ahmed Aboul Gheit, who greeted me in a similar manner when I took up my post at the UN, visiting me rather than the other way around. My friendship with Alessandro continued through the years. At the time of our first meeting, I was unaware of his iconic efforts to get the partnership between the Gulf countries and NATO off the ground. He also shared with me that the Kuwait Embassy was formerly the NATO Secretary-General's residence until it was relocated for security reasons. This meant that I was spending long hours in the SG's former bedroom! I partook in NATO's Annual Conference on Arms Control, Disarmament and Weapons of Mass Destruction Non-Proliferation, where I spoke five times, thanks to previous collaboration with colleagues at the UN. The topic fascinated me, and I prided myself on being an accessible participant compared to the others. The organization had to appreciate the fact that there was a credibility issue. While its basic policy is nuclear deterrence, the thrust towards non-proliferation in other regions has to stand the test. Likewise, I was of the opinion that prodding other nations to be a part of arms control conventions had to be the norm for members of the organization themselves. At one of these conferences where I was a speaker, I raised the issue of the credibility of NATO to espouse non-proliferation when NATO's very strategy is based on the importance of nuclear deterrence.

I enjoyed liaising with NATO and believed close collaboration with the members was an asset in Kuwait's efforts towards greater security. I was gratified to facilitate the passage of the Transit of Forces agreement, though it was finalized after I left my post in Brussels.

In 2011 I was officially nominated as the Representative of the State of Kuwait to NATO. That was in line with a new policy by the organization to open the door to "partner states," or countries for full-fledged representation. Unfortunately, my credentials were not even considered, as there was a so-called soft moratorium on the issue due to a standoff between Turkey, a NATO member, and Israel, a "partner" country. The issue was eventually resolved after the two countries resolved their

differences over the Gaza flotilla raid of 2010. My colleague
Jasem Albudaiwi would be appointed Kuwait's first Ambassador to NATO just a few years later.

Belgium and Luxembourg

While the European Union and NATO both offer a multilateral experience and their own unique challenge, I still had
bilateral duties to attend to in the Kingdom of Belgium. During
the Kuwaiti Prime Minister's visit in 2007, I managed to
arrange a private meeting over tea between His Highness and
then Crown Prince Philippe at the latter's residence, discreetly
avoiding any media coverage. This encounter provided a
unique glimpse into the Royal Court, showcasing the delicate
balance between official protocol and informal diplomacy.

My engagement with the Royal Court extended beyond
improvised meetings, involving the facilitation of a visit to
Kuwait by Princess Astrid, a patron of "Roll Back Malaria"[5],
an organization which is committed to coordinated action
towards ending malaria. A memorable token from the visit was
a mosquito net, a practical gift that found utility in my outdoor
activities and was something that I could have used in some of
my earlier postings in Africa.

The latter part of my stay in Brussels was marked by
personal concerns as my mother's health deteriorated in early
2012. I was visiting home on every available occasion and felt
torn when I had to be back in Brussels. I was on such a leave

---

5   endmalaria.org

when she passed away peacefully in her sleep. I had spent that night lying fully dressed in my bed, only to be woken up to the fact that she was no more. I felt a great emptiness that would only be soothed by time.

A notable development during my tenure in Brussels was the visit to Kuwait by the Minister of Foreign Affairs at the time, Didier Reynders, in December 2012. This trip marked a shift from one-way visits by Kuwaiti officials. I was gratified by the outcomes of the visit, which included the promotion of scientific collaboration, specifically in the field of solar energy, among cooperation in other fields.

One evening, while I was at a dinner in Brussels, I noticed a Kuwaiti decoration on the chest of one of the officers. Upon further inquiry, I learned that the officer was in fact Rear-Admiral Jean Paul Robyns of the Belgian navy, who had led the coalition's navy vessels in demining Kuwaiti waters during the Gulf War. It was a pleasant surprise, and I resolved to keep in contact with him and his team from the early 1990s. Later on I took the opportunity to host a dinner in honor of the officers and all of their partners. Keen to have Kuwait recognize the Belgian navy's contribution, I secured an invitation by the Ministry of Defense to invite the Rear-Admiral and his team for a visit to the country in 2010. We even managed to sneak his wife into the delegation by listing her as an officer instead of a spouse!

Belgium is also the headquarters of Q8 (Kuwait Petroleum International) activity in the Benelux (Belgium, Netherlands, Luxembourg). Initially Q8's relationship with the embassy was cordial; however, it became much closer following a welcome change in the administrative setup of their office when a Kuwaiti national assumed the helm.

We assisted Q8 in its endeavor to acquire a service station on a major highway junction connecting Luxembourg to Belgium, France, and Germany. I made it a point to relentlessly include the issue in my meetings with the authorities in Luxembourg, referring to it as "raising the flag of Kuwait in Luxembourg." Eventually, in 2014, the service station, the third largest motorway site in the world, was established. I regret being unable to be there in person to celebrate its inauguration, which took place after I left Brussels.

Just as in all of my other postings, friends and family would come to visit me in the heart of Europe. One such memorable event was when longtime friends from New York— Mary, Mia, Sonia, and Eddie—surprised me with a visit to celebrate my birthday with a group trip to the beautiful city of Bruges.

Even my departure from Brussels was not free of a little flair. I had the privilege of being the first Ambassador to meet the newly anointed King Philippe in his capacity as monarch, where he presented me with the Order of the Crown-Grand Cross. It was an unforgettable event for me. After a short tea with King Philippe, he bid farewell to me and actually escorted me to my car.

Visit by a delegation of the Kuwait National Assembly to Brussels, Belgium. Third from left: Andre Flahaut, President of Chamber of Representatives. Fourth from left: Jassem Al-Kharafi, Speaker of the Kuwait National Assembly (2011)

With Jassem Al-Kharafi, Speaker of the Kuwait National Assembly, Brussels, Belgium (2011)

Nabeela Al Mulla

*With Didier Reynders, Minister of Foreign Affairs of the
Kingdom of Belgium, during his visit to Kuwait in December
2012*

*Visiting Q8 (Kuwait Petroleum International) headquarters
in Antwerp, Belgium (2011)*

Q8 presenting me with a gift of gratitude, Brussels, Belgium (2012)

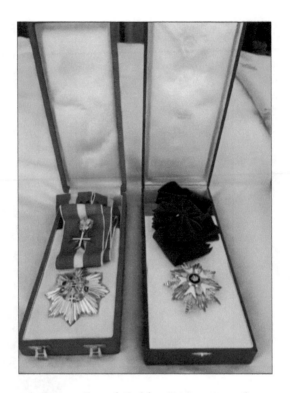

*Austrian Grand Golden Decoration of
Honor for First Class Merit (left) and
Belgian Order of the Crown-Grand Cross*

Embracing Home

It is impossible to enjoy idling thoroughly unless one has plenty of work to do. There is no fun in doing nothing when you have nothing to do.

—Jerome K. Jerome

Leaving my final posting in October 2013 as a career diplomat felt like an unanticipated twist in my life story. I would have preferred to stay on, to continue for at least a few years in the diplomatic realm that had shaped so much of my life. However, there were rules to abide by, and retirement age was one of them. It was time for me to make room for some new blood.

The transition ahead called for adaptability, and I was somewhat prepared. In a coincidental act of foreshadowing months before my departure from Brussels, my brother had shown me an unassuming office within our family business compound. "This is for you Nabeela," he said. "You cannot be in the Ministry forever." As it turned out, this office would become my niche, a pied-à-terre in the next phase of my life. To this day, I continue to enjoy this space, as it fills me with a sense of attachment and stability.

At the outset, I envisioned my stay in Kuwait as temporary. I had witnessed how leading figures often ended up in academia or think-tanks, and I imagined myself doing the same. My plan was to seek association with an academic institution abroad, where I could share my diplomatic experiences and insights with a wider audience. Meanwhile, the idea of penning my own narrative slowly took root. Having lived primarily in the Western world, I appreciated the importance of recording one's life journey, but in those days, the writing of autobiographies and memoirs—especially by our elders in the Gulf—was not the norm. I could not help but fault them for not documenting their rich life experiences. Fortunately, over the past few years, I've seen more memoirs from the region, albeit with a caveat: Most of the literature is still in Arabic, limiting its circulation. While I mulled over how to approach my own memoir, I maintained my contacts and participated in events as a speaker, particularly on issues of security and non-proliferation. I was unburdened by officialdom, yet found myself in parallel with mainstream thinking at home. Even then, I continued to fault some of the events I attended as mere echo chambers, where ideas bounced around without creating any meaningful impact or growth.

That said, my first foray into the post-Foreign Ministry life set the bar high for future interactions. I was appreciative of the Kuwait Foundation for the Advancement of Sciences (KFAS) and its Director-General Dr. Adnan, a former colleague, for their support in facilitating one of my first experiences as a guest lecturer in the spring of 2014. Upon the invitation by Ambassador Nicholas Burns, who was then the Faculty Chair of the Middle East Initiative and Kuwait Program at Harvard University's Kennedy School, I participated in a well-attended public talk focusing on the international developments in the region. The event mainly centered on the JCPOA, Iran, and the Gulf, and it included a dinner with other guests hosted by Ambassador Burns at the Harvard Faculty Club.

With Ambassador Nicholas Burns at Harvard University's Kennedy School (2014)

One of the highlights of my visit to Harvard for this event was the opportunity to meet with the fellows of the Managing the Atom Program at the Belfer Center for Science and International Affairs. Their curiosity about my tenure as the Chair of the IAEA Board of Governors in 2002–2003 sparked engaging discussions. At that gathering, I met fellows hailing from Singapore, Iran, New Zealand, and the United States, among others. I also had the chance to reconnect with Laura, a former colleague from my time with the IAEA, and Olli, another former colleague, whose insights about Harvard were interesting. They highlighted the nuanced differences between the way professionals in the field and those of academia worked.

It was during this contemplative phase that a friend, Samer, suggested I consider joining academia in Kuwait. While this was a compelling idea, I still clamored for pastures abroad and sought and secured association with Oxford University as an Academic Visitor to St. Antony's College. I thoroughly enjoyed my stint at Oxford, returning on multiple occasions; however, the restrictions of their two-year status served as a stark reminder that my narrative needed to be penned on my own terms and in my own good time. With that in mind, I joined the American University of Kuwait in 2015 as a distinguished lecturer, collaborating with several professors in tutoring on foreign policy, international relations, and political theory. In this capacity, relaying my experiences gave students the added value of literally bringing the history in their textbooks to life, and it was invigorating for me to be around bright young minds. I recalled with satisfaction that upon my own graduation from university, I had academia in my sights, and here I was, decades later, completing the circle.

With the president of the American University of Kuwait, Dr. Nizar Hamza, Kuwait City, Kuwait (2015)

During this time, I also continued my engagement in non-proliferation and geopolitics through my participation in various conferences and seminars. I was invited to speak at an EU consortium on the Comprehensive Test Ban Treaty in 2015. I took part in the Annual NATO Conference on Arms Control, Disarmament and WMD Non-Proliferation in Interlaken, Ljubljana, and Reykjavik in 2014, 2016, and 2018, respectively. I participated in the Amman Nuclear Forum in 2017 and was invited to the Oman National Defense College to speak about security issues and my experience at the UN. Another forum I was involved in was a conference in Istanbul hosted by the International Institute for Strategic Studies that focused on geopolitical security issues in the Middle East, under the guidance of Mark Fitzpatrick, a former colleague from my days in Vienna.

With Thomas Countryman, US Assistant Secretary for International Security and Non-proliferation, at an EU consortium on the Comprehensive Test Ban Treaty (2015)

Visit to the Oman Defense College, Muscat, Oman. Left to right: Head of the Defense College, me, and Ambassador Ghazi Al Rawas, a former colleague from Brussels (2015)

*With officials from the Oman Defense College, Muscat, Oman
(2015)*

My retirement offered me more time to pursue activities
that I was unable to do while I was Ambassador. This included
supporting the nonprofit SOS Children's Villages, a non-
governmental organization focused on supporting children
without parental care and families at risk. I was introduced
to this noble project by a lifelong friend, Afifa, who at the
time was President of the organization's chapter in Lebanon.
Their objective of finding a home for every child in their own
community was a cause that everyone in my family, particularly
my late mother, identified strongly with. I visited some of their
"villages" where they housed Lebanese and Syrian orphans as

well as their main "village" in Innsbruck, Austria. Touched, I took it upon myself to facilitate contact between this organization and donors in Kuwait, for which SOS's former renowned President, the late Helmut Kutin, bestowed upon me their Golden Badge of Honor in 2014.

While the COVID-19 pandemic impacted my activities, it did not halt them. Back when I served as the Chairman of the Board of Governors in 2002, I facilitated the establishment of the Cooperative Agreement for Arab States in Asia for Research Development and Training Related to Nuclear Science and Technology (ARASIA). Despite Kuwait not being an initial signatory member, I strongly believed in the incremental value of encouraging cooperation between Arab states and the IAEA. During the COVID pandemic, I was contacted by a former Kuwaiti colleague, who informed me that ARASIA was going to be celebrating the 20th anniversary of its establishment. They wanted me to participate in the event, which I did, remotely. It is deeply gratifying to have been able to witness the evolution of ARASIA into a viable and effective entity. The skepticism that once surrounded its inception has been replaced by tangible achievements and collaborative successes. Another circle completed.

It was also during the pandemic that the Woodrow Wilson Center contacted me as part of their ACRS Oral History project. They conducted a number of off- and on-the-record interviews with diplomats and officials who participated in the ACRS multilateral meetings back in the early 1990s. It seems the ACRS would be a darling reference for politicians and think-tanks to draw the way forward for zones free of weapons of mass destruction, and the interviews, including mine, are freely available in a digital archive on the Woodrow Wilson Center's website.

Around the same time, I was surprised when I was selected by Secretary-General of the United Nations António Guterres to join his Advisory Board on Disarmament Matters. I could not help but reflect on my humble beginnings as a young woman in 1978, attending the first Special Session on Disarmament at the UN, which had authorized the establishment of such an advisory board. I recall being so enamored by the presence of Paul Newman in the American delegation that I walked up to him, introduced myself, and let him know that his blue eyes had already left me disarmed. Joining the Advisory Board was a thrilling return to the mainstream, a place where my voice and experience could impact decision-making. This honor was repeated and renewed for an additional two-year term, and another part of my life had come full circle.

In this new chapter of my life, I often find myself reflecting on all the lessons and experiences of my diplomatic journey. Those reflections bring to mind a quotation from novelist Haruki Murakami: "People's memories are maybe the fuel they burn to stay alive." My transition away from official diplomatic posts has had its share of surprises and uncertainties, but my memories confirm that every curve in the road, every unexpected destination, and every Plan B can offer as much enrichment and fulfillment as one's unrealized plans might have provided, if not more.

Plaque honoring my mother at SOS Children's Villages in Lebanon (2017)

A meeting between the President of SOS Children's Villages (fourth from left) and Dr. Abdlatif Al-Hamad (third from left), Secretary General of the Arab Fund for Economic and Social Development in Kuwait City (2014)

Helmut Kutin, President of SOS, presenting me with the Golden Badge of Honor (2014)

ACKNOWLEDGEMENTS

As I reflect on the many trials and successes that have shaped my journey, spanning continents and cultures, one constant has remained: the unwavering support of my family and friends. It is with a heart full of gratitude that I acknowledge their profound impact on my life and career.

I was advised that my memoir should be about my own personal experience, which is a unique one that highlights how I dealt with well-documented historical events. This memoir is as much a testament to the love and support of my family and friends as it is a chronicle of my journey. Every page, every memory, and every achievement is intertwined with their presence.

From the early steps, navigating the intricacies of international assignments, to the heights of my diplomatic achievements, my family and friends have been my rock. Their encouragement and support has provided me the strength to face challenges head-on, their wisdom has guided me through difficult decisions, and their love has been a sanctuary in times of uncertainty. I have often drawn upon their faith in me to persevere through moments of doubt and to celebrate achievements, both big and small.

To all who have walked this path with me, your impact has been immeasurable. I am deeply grateful for each and every one of you, in particular those who advised me on this manuscript: Afifa, Amal, Anwar, Avi, Madani, Mary, Samer, Sami, and Sonia.

ANNEX

- Three letters from my late brother Bader Al Mulla, State Secretary of Kuwait, to the Secretary-General and the President of the UN Security Council, June–July 1961

- "The Denuclearization of the Middle East," my American University of Beirut (AUB) draft resolution, excerpt of pages 73-74, early 1970s

- Personal invitation to me from His Excellency Ahmed bin Khalifa Al-Suwaidi, first Minister of Foreign Affairs of the United Arab Emirates, 1974

- "Implementation of the NPT safeguards agreement in the Islamic Republic of Iran." Excerpt from statement I delivered at Board of Governors meeting on 19 June 2003 urging Iran to cooperate.

- "The humanitarian crisis in Syria," an article I wrote for *New Europe*, February 2013

Letter dated 4 July 1961 from the Secretary-General to the President of the Security Council

[Original text: English]
[5 July 1961]

I have the honour to bring to your attention the following telegram addressed to me on 4 July 1961:

"In accordance with the item regarding Kuwait which is now under consideration by the Security Council, I have the honour to request the Council to invite the Representative of Kuwait to participate in discussion. I hereby authorize Mr. Abdel Aziz Hussein to represent Kuwait in the discussion. *(Signed)* Bader Al Mulla, State Secretary of Kuwait."

(Signed) Dag HAMMARSKJOLD
*Secretary-General of the
United Nations*

Lettre, en date du 4 juillet 1961, adressée par le Secrétaire général au Président du Conseil de sécurité

[Texte original en anglais]
[5 juillet 1961]

J'ai l'honneur de porter à votre attention le télégramme ci-après qui m'a été adressé le 4 juillet 1961:

« S'agissant de la question relative au Koweït dont le Conseil de sécurité est actuellement saisi, j'ai l'honneur de prier le Conseil d'inviter le représentant du Koweït à participer à la discussion. J'habilite par la présente M. Abdel Aziz Hussein à représenter le Koweït au cours de la discussion. *(Signé)* Bader Al Mulla, secrétaire d'État du Koweït. »

*Le Secrétaire général
de l'Organisation des Nations Unies,
(Signé)* Dag HAMMARSKJOLD

Letter dated 30 June 1961 from the State Secretary of Kuwait to the Secretary-General

[Original text: English]
[6 July 1961]

On behalf of the Government of Kuwait and in my capacity as State Secretary, I have the honour to inform you that Kuwait, an independent State, wishes herewith to make application for membership of the United Nations, with all the rights and the duties attaching thereto, and I should accordingly be grateful if this application could be submitted to the Security Council at its nearest meeting. For this purpose, I am sending under separate cover, a declaration made by the Head of our State pursuant to rule 58 of the Council's provisional rules of procedures.

(Signed) Bader AL MULLA
State Secretary of Kuwait

Lettre, en date du 30 juin 1961, adressée au Secrétaire général par le Secrétaire d'État du Koweït

[Texte original en anglais]
6 juillet 1961]

Au nom du Gouvernement du Koweït et en ma qualité de Secrétaire d'État, j'ai l'honneur de vous faire savoir que l'État indépendant du Koweït désire demander par les présentes son admission à l'Organisation des Nations Unies, avec tous les droits et obligations qui en découlent; je vous serais donc reconnaissant de bien vouloir soumettre cette demande au Conseil de sécurité à sa prochaine séance. A cette fin, je vous envoie, sous pli séparé, la déclaration faite par le chef de l'État, conformément à l'article 58 du règlement intérieur provisoire du Conseil.

*Le Secrétaire d'État du Koweït,
(Signé)* Bader AL MULLA

DECLARATION

I, the Ruler of Kuwait, have the honour to declare, in connexion with the application by the Government of Kuwait for membership of the United Nations, that Kuwait accepts the obligations in the Charter of the United Nations and solemnly undertakes to fulfil them.

(Signed) Abdullah AL SALIM AL SABAH
Emir of Kuwait

DÉCLARATION

En ma qualité de souverain du Koweït, j'ai l'honneur de déclarer, à l'occasion de la demande d'admission de l'État du Koweït à l'Organisation des Nations Unies, que le Koweït accepte les obligations de la Charte des Nations Unies et s'engage solennellement à les respecter.

*L'émir de Koweït,
(Signé)* Abdullah AL SALIM AL SABAH

Document S/4852: Letter from my late brother Bader Al Mulla, State Secretary of Kuwait, to the Secretary-General, 30 June 1961

UNITED NATIONS
SECURITY
COUNCIL

Distr.
GENERAL

S/4844
1 July 1961

ORIGINAL: ENGLISH

**CABLE DATED 1 JULY 1961 FROM THE STATE SECRETARY OF KUWAIT
ADDRESSED TO THE PRESIDENT OF THE SECURITY COUNCIL**

I am instructed by His Highness the Ruler of Kuwait and in accordance with paragraph two of Article 35 of the United Nations Charter, I have the honour to request you, in your capacity as President of the Security Council, to call a meeting of the Council to consider urgently the following question: "Complaint by Kuwait in respect of the situation arising from threats by Iraq to the territorial independence of Kuwait which is likely to endanger the maintenance of international peace and security".

(Signed) Bader AL MULLA
State Secretary

Letter from my late brother Bader Al Mulla, State Secretary of Kuwait, to president of the UN Security Council, 1 July 1961

UNITED NATIONS
SECURITY
COUNCIL

Distr.
GENERAL

S/4851
5 July 1961

ORIGINAL: ENG

LETTER DATED 4 JULY 1961 FROM THE SECRETARY-GENERAL ADDRESSED TO
THE PRESIDENT OF THE SECURITY COUNCIL

I have the honour to bring to your attention the following cable dated
4 July 1961:

"Honourable Dag Hammarskjold,
Secretary-General
United Nations Organization

"In accordance with the item regarding Kuwait which is now
under consideration by the Security Council, I have the honour
to request the Council to invite the Representative of Kuwait to
participate in discussion. I hereby authorize Mr. Abdel Aziz Hussein
to represent Kuwait in the discussion.

Bader Al Mulla
State Secretary"

Accept, etc.

(Signed)   Dag HAMMARSKJOLD
Secretary-General

*Letter from my late brother Bader Al Mulla, State Secretary
of Kuwait, to Dag Hammarskjold, Secretary-General of the
United Nations, 4 July 1961*

PROPOSED GENERAL ASSEMBLY RESOLUTION FOR THE DENUCLEARIZATION OF THE MIDDLE EAST

The General Assembly,

Believing in the vital necessity of saving contemporary and future generations from the scourge of nuclear war,

Recalling its resolution 2028 (XX) of 19 November 1965 on the non-proliferation of nuclear weapons,

Recalling further with satisfaction the Treaty on the Non-Proliferation of Nuclear Weapons,

Mindful of Security Council resolution 242 of 22 November 1967,

Mindful further of attempts to reach a political settlement to the Middle East conflict,

Concerned however about the political stalemate, and the possible spread of nuclear weapons,

Observing that proposals for the establishment of denuclearized zones in various areas of the world have met with general approval,

Believing that the denuclearization of various areas of the world would help to achieve the desired goal of prohibiting the use of nuclear weapons,

Recognizing that the denuclearization of the Middle East would be a practical step towards the prevention of the further spread of nuclear weapons and towards the achievement of the objectives of the United Nations,

1. Calls upon the States in the Middle East not to manufacture or use nuclear weapons, nuclear explosive devices or means of delivery; not to receive or seek assistance in the manufacture or use of nuclear weapons, nuclear explosive devices or means of delivery; and not to encourage or authorize the manufacture or use of nuclear weapons, nuclear explosive devices or means of delivery;

My American University of Beirut (AUB) draft resolution, "The Denuclearization of the Middle East," Appendix I, p. 73 (early 1970s) (continued on next page)

2.Calls upon the States in the Middle East not to seek or accept the emplacement of nuclear weapons, nuclear explosive devices or means of delivery; and to prohibit and prevent the receipt, storage, installation and deployment of nuclear weapons, nuclear explosive devices or means of delivery;

3.Calls upon the States in the Middle East not to seek or accept control in whatever form, directly or indirectly, of nuclear weapons, nuclear explosive devices or means of delivery; and to prohibit and prevent the control in whatever form, directly or indirectly, of nuclear weapons, nuclear explosive devices or means of delivery on their territory;

4.Urges all States not to disseminate information, components or material necessary for the manufacture or use of nuclear weapons, nuclear explosive devices or means of delivery; and not to encourage the States in the Middle East to manufacture or use nuclear weapons, nuclear explosive devices or means of delivery;

5.Urges all States not to store, install or deploy, in whatever form, nuclear weapons, nuclear explosive devices or means of delivery;

6.Urges all States not to assist, or induce the States in the Middle East to share control, in whatever form directly or indirectly, of nuclear weapons, nuclear explosive devices or means of delivery; and not to relinquish control over nuclear weapons, nuclear explosive devices or means of delivery to the States in the Middle East;

7.Invites the States in the Middle East to avail themselves of the assistance and services of the IAEA for the implementation of the present resolution;

8.Invites further the Secretary-General, in consultation with the Governments of the States in the Middle East, to render whatever advice and assistance may be appropriate to facilitate the implementation of the present resolution.

*Draft resolution "The Denuclearization of the Middle East,"
Appendix I, p. 74 (continued from previous page)*

دَولة الامَارات العَربيّة المتحدة
وزارة الخَارجيّة
الادارة العامة للشؤون السياسية
ــ قسم الابحاث ــ

الرقم : ٥٦ ٢٨٥ جـ ١/١/٧
التاريخ :
الموافق : ٦٦/١١/١٩٧٤م

بشأن :

حضرة الانسة نبيله البلا
وزارة الخارجيـة ــ الكويت

بعد التحية . .
ان دولة الامارات العربية المتحدة هي دولة ناشئة ، نالت استقلالها
مؤخرا ، ومنذ اليوم الاول للاستقلال ، ونحن نحاول بكل ما لدينا من جهـــد
بناء اجهزة حديثة قادرة على تحمل ها العمل والمسؤولية .

ونظرا لحاجتنا الماسة في وزارة الخارجية الى د بلوماسيين نشطيـن
فقد قمنا في الاعوام الماضية بارسال مجموعة من د بلوماسيينا لحضور د ورات ـــ
تدريبية في الخارج ، والى جانب ادارة لدورات تدريبية في داخل الوزارة . ونود
هذا العام ان نقوم بدعوة مجموعة من المهتمين بالقضايا السياسية لقضا* فتـــرة
قصيرة من الوقت معنا .

ويسرنا جدا ان تتفضلوا بزيارتنا للتحدث امامنا حول : (تحديـــد
الشرق الاوسط نوويا) وذلك يوم الاربعا* الموافق ٩/٤/١٩٧٥ .

راجين ان يكون هذا التاريخ مناسبا لكم ، ونحن على علم بكثرة مشاغلكم
وضيق وقتكم . الا اننا نأمل في ان تتمكنوا من قبول هذه الدعوة وقضا* بضعة ايام
معنا في دولة الامارات العربية المتحدة .

وستقوم سفارتنا في الكويت بتقديم ما تحتاجونه من تذاكر سفر وسمـــة
د خول . اما في ابوظبي فستعملون ضيوفنا على الدولة .
على امل لقائكم في ابوظبي اتمنى لكم العمر والعافية .

المخلـــــص
. احمد خليفه السـويـدى
وزير الخارجيّة

لنسخة طبق الى :
سفارتنا في الكويت
الادارة المالية والادارية
اللجنة المشرفة على الدورة
قسم الابحاث
الملف .

Personal invitation to me from His Excellency Ahmed bin Khalifa Al-Suwaidi, first Minister of Foreign Affairs of the United Arab Emirates, inviting me to speak at a panel in the Foreign Ministry in Abu Dhabi on denuclearizing the Middle East, 1974

181

CHAIRMAN'S CONCLUSION ON ITEM 6(b)

Implementation of the NPT safeguards agreement in the Islamic Republic of Iran:

Report by the Director General

I intend, with your permission, to wrap up our discussion on item 6 (b).

It is my understanding that the Board agrees that the Report of the Director General contained in document GOV/2003/40 be made public. I further propose that the initial statements made by Iran on Wednesday also be made public.

All statements made during the debate will be duly reflected in the summary records of our meeting.

On the basis of our discussions, I am confident that I express the broad sense of the Board in stating the following points:

The Board expressed its appreciation for the 6 June report of the Director General, which provides a factual and objective description of developments since March in relation to safeguards issues in the Islamic Republic of Iran, which need to be clarified, and actions that need to be taken.

The Board commended the Secretariat for the extensive verification activities which it has undertaken and expressed full support for its on-going efforts to resolve outstanding questions. The Board shared the concern expressed by the Director General in his report at the number of Iran's past failures to report material, facilities and activities as required by its safeguards obligations. Noting the Iranian actions taken thus far to correct these failures, the Board urged Iran promptly to rectify all safeguards problems identified in the report and resolve questions that remain open.

Board of Governors meeting statement I delivered, 19 June 2003 (continued on next page)

The Board welcomed Iran's reaffirmed commitment to full transparency and expected Iran to grant the Agency all access deemed necessary by the Agency in order to create the necessary confidence in the international community. Noting that the enrichment plant is under IAEA safeguards, the Board encouraged Iran, pending the resolution of related outstanding issues, not to introduce nuclear material at the pilot enrichment plant, as a confidence-building measure.

The Board called on Iran to co-operate fully with the Agency in its on-going work. Specifically, the Board took note of the Director General's 16 June Introductory Statement which called on Iran to permit the Agency to take environmental samples at the particular location where allegations about enrichment activities exists.

The Board welcomed Iran's readiness to look positively at signing and ratifying an additional protocol, and urged Iran to promptly and unconditionally conclude and implement an additional protocol to its Safeguards Agreement, in order to enhance the Agency's ability to provide credible assurances regarding the peaceful nature of Iran's nuclear activities, particularly the absence of undeclared material and activities.

The Board requested the Director General to provide a further report on the situation whenever appropriate.

Is the above summary acceptable?

It is so decided.

In the spirit of transparency exemplified by our colleague, Ambassador Salehi of Iran, I propose that the Chairman's concluding summary be made public.

It is so decided.

Board of Governors meeting statement (continued from previous page)

NEW EUROPE
www.neurope.eu
3 - 9 February, 2013

By Ambassador Nabeela Al Mulla

Nabeela Al Mulla is
the Ambassador of the
State of Kuwait to the
Kingdom of Belgium
and the Grand Duchy
of Luxembourg and
Head of the Mission of
the State of Kuwait to
the European Union

The humanitarian crisis in Syria

How it all started

There is a marked shortage of food, water, shelter and medical supplies. People live in a constant state of fear.

By Ambassador Nabeela Al Mulla

Nabeela Al Mulla is
the Ambassador of the
State of Kuwait to the
Kingdom of Belgium
and the Grand Duchy
of Luxembourg and
Head of the Mission of
the State of Kuwait to
the European Union

Article I wrote for New Europe *periodical on "The humanitarian crisis in Syria," February 2013*

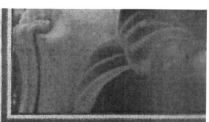

How did it start? Why is there a humanitarian crisis? It was Mohammad, a teenage boy, his friends and an afternoon of fun in Deraa in March 2011, which involved defacing a wall with graffiti. All it took were two phrases: "the people want the regime to fall" and "it's your turn doctor." The reaction was immediate. Mohammed and his friends were taken into custody where they were tortured and beaten. Word spread quickly through the tight-knit town causing family members, friends and neighbors to demand their release. President Bashar Al-Assad tried to diffuse the situation by ordering the release of Mohammed and his friends. It was too little too late. Discontent spread and eventually evolved into a bloody internal conflict with serious regional fallout. The situation has deteriorated into a humanitarian crisis let alone a political stalemate.

There are over four million people in need of humanitarian assistance, including two million internally displaced persons of which 400,000 are Palestinian refugees. The use of heavy arms is obliterating neighborhoods and causing ever increasing casualties, recently estimated at over 60,000. There is a marked shortage of food, water, shelter and medical supplies. People live in a constant state of fear. Scores of refugees have fled to the surrounding countries with Jordan, Turkey and Lebanon hosting the majority and more keep pouring in everyday. They are doing their best to provide basic services to the Syrian refugees. Their efforts have been nothing short of extraordinary. However, Jordan and Lebanon in particular have fragile infrastructures and are in dire need of assistance.

Alarming figures and facts, which were documented by specialized international agencies, all point to the future of Syria and the Syrian people looking extremely grim. Amid mounting concerns of the growing humanitarian crisis and lack of funds to address the issue the Secretary General of the United Nations requested that Kuwait host an international conference on humanitarian aid for Syria. His Highness the Emir of Kuwait welcomed the idea. This conference, which took place on 30 January 2013 and known as the International Humanitarian Pledging Conference for Syria, was intended to address the $1.5 billion funding shortfall in humanitarian aid. It is considered the largest humanitarian pledging conference in the history of the United Nations. Prior to the conference the Office for the Coordination of Human Affairs (OCHA) estimated that only 3% of this funding had already been met and that achieving the rest was imperative if services are to continue for the next six months. His Highness, who hosted the event, set the mood off to a good start by announcing a Kuwaiti donation of $300 million. He stated that, "The UN and particularly the Security Council, which is the body entrusted with the maintenance of international peace and security, are required, after almost two years to hurry, pull their ranks together and overcome some of the disappointing positions, to find a quick solution for this tragedy." His remarks were echoed by the Secretary General who said that "as we search for a political solution, we must do everything we can now to help our fellow human beings who are suffering and dying before our eyes." The United Arab Emirates and Saudi Arabia announced their own $300 million donation, which effectively raised 60% of the targeted amount of aid between the three Gulf Countries. The European Union itself pledged €100 ($135) million with individual member countries making separate donations as well. The United States offered $155 million. All of those pledges are over and above what was previously contributed. This conference was preceded by a meeting in Kuwait City of over 77 local, regional and international charity organizations, including private donors, which announced a $183 million contribution.

How will it end?

(Continued from previous page)